Echoes of Women's Tears

A 21st CENTURY GENOCIDE IN THE FORMER
BRITISH SOUTHERN CAMEROONS

Compiled By:

Dr. Patience Abiedu

Co-Authored By:

Patience Abiedu

Emma Endeley

Rachael Itah-Tima

Mary Muma

Elizabeth E. Jambelele

Gertrude Kisob

Comfort Konfor

Delavil Lekunze

Ma Mado

Dorothy Mofor

Anne Ndeh

Marianta Ndoh Njomia

Dorothy Ngwa

Irene Ngwa

Martha Shey

Victorine Yangni

Dedication

This book is dedicated to the brave men, women, and children who have paid the ultimate price for our freedom.

Acknowledgments

We would like to acknowledge the immense contributions made by several comrades, friends, and associates of the Southern Cameroons (Ambazonia) in these trying and difficult times of our quest for independence. We are particularly grateful to Mr. Clifford Marcussen, Rev. Pat Hightower, Mrs. Judith Wong, Mrs. Sheila Alston, Dr. Emma Osong, Barrister Valentine Gana, Dr. Joseph Takang, Dr. Nicoline Ambe, and Dr. Julius Abiedu for their input, encouragement, and support in the publication of this book. Finally, we are grateful to Dr. Patience Abiedu for conceptualizing this project in March of 2018 as well as for Ma Mary Muma for editing this masterpiece.

THANK YOU.

TABLE OF CONTENTS

Editor's Note

By Mary Muma

Women remain disproportionately affected by the war waged on the Southern Cameroons (also known as Ambazonia) by Paul Biya and the Cameroonian government. An idea was proposed for their voices to be heard through a permanent testament. This collection of short stories and reflections is the breath behind those voices.

As editor, my role was not only to tie these women's stories and reflections together, but also to inform you, our esteemed readers, and to bring to life even the most painful experiences of loss, trauma, devastation, and even death perpetrated by president Biya's regime. My role was rewarding because of the opportunity to continue our struggle on these literary pages. It was also challenging because I had to ensure that the writers' voices were heard as they intended, and that the emotions they intend to generate strike the necessary moral chords in our esteemed readers. Therefore, the preservation of their style, tone, and message was paramount. For conciseness, some changes have been made. Any lapses on my part, or inaccuracies, are inadvertent.

I am in awe of the stories and poems in this collection, which are a response to how the women became involved in the Southern Cameroons/Ambazonia struggle for the restoration of its independence. The beauty of their drafts is that, in answering this question, they also delineate why they entered the struggle and the effects it has had on them. But the sixteen women capture and chronicle the struggle in the punchiest, detailed, and engaging of ways for our benefit.

Editor's Note

The styles of the writers are as diverse as the genres in this collection – narrative fiction fused into poetry, fused into letters and history, our history. So, it is a compelling read, and the reader is orientated by the writers at every opportunity.

The tone of this piece is pervasively somber but gives the impression that the women's happiness has just been delayed, reserved for Freedom Celebration Day when it arrives. The themes involve desperation, lamentation, loss, anguish, hopelessness, restlessness, freedom, struggle, and hope - hence the "Echoes of Women's Tears."

The stories are crafted to shock the reader out of complacency, indecision, insensitivity, and depravity, and to push them to embrace empathy and decisive action – to call for an end to the war and a restoration of our independence. These stories are the 'get up' needed for the world to act in stopping Biya's genocide in our homeland. I salute the women's courage, directness, and creativity. By coming out in Ambazonia's desperate moment of need, they achieve the status of literary Takembengs. Something terrible is befalling our homeland! The women in this collection have therefore risen in defense of motherland in a way which only they know best.

CHAPTER 1

A CHANGE OF HEART: FROM A UNITARIST TO A RESTORATIONIST

PATIENCE ABIEDU

Are you not afraid of what could happen to you when you visit Cameroon?" a family member asked me in October 2018. It was just another day for me, except that my life now had a new dimension and energy. My family was worried and rightfully so.

I replied, "I will not be visiting La Republique du Cameroun (LRC). I will return to the Southern Cameroons someday, God willing. There was a smile on my face and determination in my voice. Inside, I felt a jolt of fear and doubt sweeping over me. Could my dream of a sovereign nation really come to pass? Could it be that one day I would go back home to the Southern Cameroons, a country free from the clutches of LRC? Suffice to say, I have not dared to return to that place where I grew up called La Republique du Cameroun, or in English, "The Republic of Cameroon." I am certain that doing so would be a one-way ticket to one of the country's dungeons (if I am lucky), or even my demise. And that holds true for millions of Ambazonians around the world, now refugees, escapees from economic annihilation, or certain political death. Like me, they have all woken up to a new reality.

You see, I was not always a "restorationist"—or by definition, a

1

supporter of an independent "West Cameroon." So-called West Cameroon, my homeland, has been given a plethora of names—and is sometimes referred to as the "former British Trust Territory of the Southern Cameroons," and more recently, "Northwest and Southwest Regions," "NOSO," "Special Status" region, or whatever new labels LRC[1] ascribes to us. I was born and raised to believe in a certain Cameroon—a 'federated' then 'unitary state that came into sovereignty on January 1, 1960. It was simply the Cameroon I had grown up in. Like many of my peers, I never quite grasped why there was always such an uneasy feeling about being Anglophone Cameroonian. We were children caught up in the farce that is Cameroon - LRC. We have woken up to a new but very odd realization that for 60 years, we have been sold merchandise composed of lies. I have been comfortable with the familiar. It was nothing new to say I was an "Anglophone" or to learn that the country had a name change. In fact, there have been several name changes in the course of my 57 years. It is sufficient to say that I did not espouse the notion that LRC and the former British Southern Cameroons should be two separate nations. That did not sit well with me for several reasons. The most obvious was that I was comfortable with what I was familiar with, which was Anglophone families and Francophone families co-existing in peace. However, as an adult, I realize that this "peace" was illusive. Anglophone Cameroonians had been disenfranchised and disempowered from the very onset of the unification of the Southern Cameroons and La Republique du Cameroun.

Thus, my desire to see a unified Cameroon eventually changed.

---

[1] LRC: abbreviation for La Republique du Cameroon, a French translation of "The Republic of Cameroon". Also commonly considered to be the French-speaking side of Cameroon.

Several events in 2016 stirred a strong desire to fight for my people in a way that still surprises me today. The events linked to the Southern Cameroonian teachers' and lawyers' protests in late 2016 marked the beginning of the end of our lives in servitude to LRC. As if the arrests and beatings suffered by the teachers and lawyers were not enough, gasoline was poured on our wounds when Ambazonian activist, Mancho Bibixy and hundreds of young men who took to the streets in peaceful protest for basic social amenities (like good roads and infrastructure) were brutally rounded up and attacked by the military – sadly resulting in some deaths. Those who cheated death were carted off to dungeons in LRC. LRC's President Paul Biya ignited a fire in me and many of my sisters in the Southern Cameroonian Diaspora when he declared war on "Anglophones" in November of 2017, fraudulently citing a terrorist insurrection in my homeland. That day, I became an unapologetic advocate for the restoration of Southern Cameroons' (Ambazonia) independence. Perhaps, a chronological narrative may shine further light on my developing convictions and the need to restore nationhood to Ambazonians. This chapter will include excerpts of communications that took place between January 2017 and March 2019.

When it came to the situation in my homeland, I had so many questions and concerns: How did peaceful protests, held by teachers and lawyers, morph into a government-sponsored genocide? How is it that these non-violent protests led to a scorched-earth policy where entire villages have been set ablaze, and innocent men, women, and children slaughtered? How is it that hundreds of thousands of Southern Cameroonians are now refugees in neighboring Nigeria? How did we — a free, prosperous, and proud people of the Southern Cameroons become internally displaced?

I wanted to know why my people were being chased out of their

3

ECHOES OF WOMEN'S TEARS

incinerated homes and being forced to seek refuge in forests. The thought of old men, women, and children being ruthlessly dealt with by Cameroon's Rapid Intervention Battalion Brigade (BIR) truly made no sense to me. I wanted to know where thousands of Southern Cameroonian boys, criminalized by Biya's Army, were being taken to. Could they have been accounted for in jails around the country? How many had been mercilessly killed by Biya's Army? Having none of the answers to any of these questions, I knew the only thing left to do was to fight for my people. I did not know how I would join the fight, but I was willing to try.

Thousands of miles away, in the USA, President Donald Trump began his war against what he called "illegal immigrants" and created the "Make America Great Again," (MAGA) campaign. In the early months of 2017, he issued executive orders concerning sanctuary cities, refugee admissions, and immigration bans. Trump's determination to build a wall separating the U.S. southern border from Mexico hit me like a ton of bricks. The concepts of freedom, liberty, and the pursuit of happiness began to seem elusive even from my "safe-haven" here in the U.S. "Which human being is born an illegal person?" I wondered. Didn't the forefathers of White Americans like Trump come from nations far away from this originally Native-American land? Despite my citizenship, I no longer felt at home here. My thoughts turned to Cameroon—another country where discrimination plagued my people. Neither country welcomed me. The realization that I may soon not have a place to call home began to haunt me. Something had to be done! That was the beginning of my journey.

In the early months of 2017, I invited a few leaders in my community to draft a petition to President Donald Trump. One of those leaders was my friend, Mr. Francis Shey. It was our hope that

4

Trump would read our petition and change American policies related to African countries with the goal of holding African leaders accountable for their actions. I wanted President Biya to be held accountable for his crimes and wanton attacks on a defenseless people. The following is the petition to President Trump in March 2017:

Petition to President Donald Trump

For 55 years, the people of the former British Southern Cameroons have been marginalized by the majority French-Cameroonian government currently headed by Mr. Paul Biya. As a result of this marginalization, lawyers and teachers from this region made demands through demonstrations and strike actions. The government reacted violently by sending in the army, who killed, raped, jailed, and tortured unarmed, peaceful demonstrators—including university students. These atrocious acts are still going on and if they are not stopped, this crisis may lead to another Rwanda-like genocide where more than a million of the minority population was slaughtered. To prevent the world from seeing these inhumane acts and human rights violations, the French Cameroonian government shut down the Internet and all forms of social media communication systems in the British Southern Cameroons. This is yet another example of how Southern Cameroonians have been marginalized for 55 years.

President Trump, as the leader of the free world, we are asking you to intervene and save my people from persecution and total annihilation. Something should be done to stop the killing, rape, torture, and arbitrary arrest of innocent Southern Cameroonians. We urge you to act to free all arbitrarily arrested activists of the Southern Cameroons self-determination cause; restore the Internet and social media in the Southern Cameroons. Help the people of the Southern Cameroons achieve their right to self-determination so that schools and the courts can resume normal functioning.

The calls to action in the petition are extremely important because we want peace and stability in the Southern Cameroons. Solutions to these problems would allow for a flourishing democracy, economic development, prosperity, good governance, and better quality of life. Such an environment will lead to fewer Cameroonians migrating to the United States to seek better opportunities. Free the people of former British Southern Cameroonians now—before it is too late.

Unfortunately, we did not gather the required 100,000 signatures required for President Trump and the U.S. Congress to examine our petition. But it was not a lost cause, as it generated more awareness about the plight of the Southern Cameroons (Ambazonia).

At a more local level, I reached out to California Congresswoman, Karen Bass, who serves on the U.S. House Committee on Foreign Affairs. At the time, she was a high-ranking member of the Subcommittee on Africa, Global Health, Global Human Rights, and International Organizations. Consequently, I felt that she was an important figure to speak with, particularly because in February 2017, she condemned intimidation against the English-speaking population by LRC, and urged President Biya to respect the civil and human rights of all its citizens. She also asked for an immediate end to violent attacks on protesters, including an end to Internet blackouts in Ambazonia. I was hopeful for the future, and I prayed that more U.S. officials would join Congresswoman Bass in taking a stand against the crimes committed by President Biya and his forces.

As time passed, the conditions in the Southern Cameroons worsened. The Republic of Cameroon's Army, commonly known as BIR, commenced a 'scorched-earth' approach to fighting the people of Ambazonia, burning down the homes of suspected Restoration

6

Fighters and burning down of schools and hospitals, in their attempt to quell what Mr. Biya, in his diabolical thinking described as a group of terrorists that were destabilizing his country. By 2018-2019, the security situation in all parts of Ambazonia had deteriorated to the point that most parents were scared to death to send their children to school. I remember asking myself why we could not be allowed to develop our own curriculum and teach our children in English? I guess that was wishful thinking. The petition had not delivered results as intended. But was I going to be complacent and look the other way because I was not directly involved? Not at all!

In early April 2017, a selected group of Southern Cameroonians living in Los Angeles met to discuss the horrors unfolding before our eyes on our social media and echoed in the desperate voices of our loved ones. We needed to do something. But what? The war was moving on a fast track. We invited some prominent Southern Cameroonian leaders to talk about the deteriorating situation in the Southern Cameroons and to raise funds to meet increasing needs for medical care, shelter, food, and care for the displaced. I found myself at the center of things having been the event organizing committee member. This was the very first time I donated money towards the struggle. I must admit that at this time, I felt comfortable being a federalist—a supporter of a two-state federation made up of the Southern Cameroons (Ambazonia) and LRC, the abbreviation of "La Republique du Cameroun." I thought that a two-state federation could be the solution to the marginalization of our people. I was still under the illusion of living in this place called LRC, but I now understand that our problems are far greater and can never be expressed nor understood simply as a problem of marginalization.

Every successful revolution must have the right leadership in place. As things progressed, what began as simple demands by

7

teachers and lawyers became the springboard for leaders to emerge and for a governing structure to take root. At the beginning, there was the Consortium, the umbrella organization for teachers and lawyers facing down the government of LRC to quit destroying our education system and subjecting us to legal traditions that are foreign to our people. However, those leaders were arrested and locked up in the dreaded Kondengui prison, for daring to demand equality for their homeland and exercising their right to free speech. I would later hear of the Southern Cameroons Ambazonia Consortium United Front (SCACUF). SCACUF later transformed into the Southern Cameroons Governing Council and finally to the Interim Government of the Federal Republic of Ambazonia, headed by Sisiku Julius Ayuk Tabe as the Interim President. President Sisiku Ayuk Tabe would later travel to the U.S. and Europe with a great deal of hope and optimism to meet a jubilant people, all eager to welcome and share in this magic and dream of a soon-to-be liberated Ambazonia. While I was not 100 percent supportive of the interim government around this time, I was an ardent supporter of our Independence Restoration movement. On September 22, 2017, I joined the Southern Cameroonian community of Southern California as we welcomed President Sisiku Ayuk Tabe to Los Angeles. This was the second fundraiser my Southern Cameroonian community in California had organized to support and promote our journey to freedom.

One week later, on October 1st, 2017, Sisiku Julius Ayuk Tabe declared a restored independence of The Southern Cameroons and called for everyone in our homeland to go out and celebrate this national day. It was on this day in 1961 that the nation of the former British Southern Cameroons, transitioned to an independent country, a nation free of any neo-colonial rule. The Southern Cameroons, also known as Ambazonia, was declared an autonomous

8

and self-governing state. It marked the rebirth of our nation. Looking back today, although we lost some innocent souls at the hands of Biya's army, that was a glorious day—a day that was once only a dream! The proclamation of our Independence Day reaffirmed my belief that there was no turning back for us as a people. Witnessing the rebirth of a once prosperous nation called the Southern Cameroons, has been my proudest moment in the revolution thus far.

The jubilation was short-lived. Upon his return from attending the 5th African Union-European Union Summit in Abidjan, President Biya would later declare war on Ambazonia on November 30, 2017. This was the defining moment for me. I knew that with every fiber of my being that I would be a part of the independence struggle until we gained our freedom. There was no question in my mind that I would do everything in my power to fight for the liberation of my people.

Following Biya's declaration, every Ambazonian abroad would wake up to dreadful images of burnt homes and villages, families fleeing the BIR, corpses abandoned by the roadside and others buried in mass graves, along with countless other atrocities. The killing of our people has been normalized by LRC forces who forcefully occupied our homeland.

I could not understand why the international community had been deaf to the cries of our people and the humanitarian crisis unfolding in Ambazonia. I decided to send emails to major news outlets like MSNBC, The Rachel Maddow Show, and CNN's Fareed Zakari. No one responded. So, I decided to continue to engage in the fight for freedom on a much smaller scale. Some members of the Southern Cameroonian community spent an afternoon rallying in front of Los Angeles's French Consulate in order to stand in solidarity with Southern Cameroonians all over the world. I was proud to be a part of that demonstration. However, the thought that a major genocide was going on in Ambazonia filled me with pain and anger.

More and more images of the carnage in Ambazonia began to spread on social media and I could not help but think that disaster on the scale of Rwanda's 1994 genocide was brewing. While I continued to make numerous calls to major news outlets, no major newspaper picked up any stories about the happenings in the Southern Cameroons. In fact, it seemed as if the Francophone government of Cameroon was gaining support internationally, despite their heinous crimes against innocent civilians.

As things in Ambazonia worsened, my motivation to fight even harder for my people's freedom increased, and so did my frustration with the world's silence. One morning, I awoke, and as usual, I gravitated towards my cell phone. After listening to my morning devotion, I started sifting through the hundreds of messages that had inundated my WhatsApp account. I could not believe my eyes when I came across the video of two women crying over what looked like charred human remains. I would later find out that these women were crying over the charred remains of Mami Api, a 96-year-old mother in Kwa Kwa, a Southern Cameroonian village, who was burnt alive in her home by Paul Biya's infamous Army, the BIR. Being of old age, she was not able to get out of her home when the BIR set it on fire. The video brought uncontrollable tears to my eyes and still haunts me today. Mami Api became one of the indelible symbols of the struggle to free ourselves from LRC's deadly clutches. Mami Api could have been anyone's mother, grandmother, or great-grandmother. I asked myself, "how did the Southern Cameroons get here?"

From that day on, my stance was that of a unitary state, combining the Southern Cameroons and La Republique Du Cameroun was no longer an option. It was all or nothing. Complete freedom was the only option for the Southern Cameroons. At that time, I did not know what role I would play in this liberation movement. Nonetheless, I was certain about one thing—something had to be done.

In January 2018, the Interim President Sisiku Ayuk Tabe and some of his cabinet members were abducted in Abuja, Nigeria, on the orders of dictator Paul Biya, thrown into a plane owned by the BIR, and flown into LRC. They were kept incommunicado for over 8 months in what appeared to be a dungeon. Various theories surfaced as to what had happened to them. There was so much confusion surrounding their abduction and detention that I began to grow nervous about how this would affect our fight for freedom and those involved in it. However, thanks to God, a new leadership emerged, with a man named Dr. Samuel Sako to serve as the Acting Interim President. Before taking this office, he had been a consistent voice in the struggle and was popularly known as 'Dr. Commonsense.'

One day in March, I received a WhatsApp message from a woman named Mrs. Irene Ngwa. It was concerning Dr. Sako's plan to continue the Revolution. He had a vision for our freedom to be achieved with the help of a $2 million-dollar fundraising initiative called "My Trip to Buea". The city of Buea is the capital of the Southern Cameroons and the symbol of freedom for Ambazonians. This money was aimed to help us achieve our independence and get to Buea sooner—if only we all contributed to the pot. Donating to the fund signified purchasing a symbolic ticket not only to Buea, but also to freedom. In that conversation, Mrs. Ngwa, who was the

Director of the fund, convinced me to go on a Southern Cameroonian Broadcasting Station to shed light on what the fundraiser was all about, since my husband and I had spent quite some money in purchasing our "My Trip to Buea" tickets. That was the beginning of a strong and rewarding relationship with a powerful sister in the revolution.

Not long after that, the Southern Cameroonian community in Los Angeles started planning to bring Dr. Sako to the West Coast for a major "My Trip to Buea" fundraising event. Meanwhile, thousands of miles away in French Cameroon, Barrister Akere Muna, the son of the LRC's former Prime Minister and prominent Southern Cameroonian lawyer, announced he was a candidate for the 2018 elections for the Presidency in LRC. It was troubling because I felt that with his legal background and all his international credentials, he should have been fighting to hold the Biya's administration accountable for its killings and human rights violations against Southern Cameroonians. I felt that he had no business running for office and that he had no chance of winning unless France was ready to let President Biya go. Let me hasten to add here, that I attended Barrister Muna's campaign reception in Beverly Hills and was probably the only person who was openly supportive of the Interim Government of Ambazonia. Some weeks after, Acting President Sako came to Los Angeles for a two-day fundraiser that was very successful. While I was still greatly concerned about our Interim Government leaders who were still being held incommunicado in LRC jails, it was comforting to know that our fight would continue and that we still had a chance of achieving our freedom.

I did not relent in my campaign to tell the world about the crisis in Ambazonia. From the beginning of 2017 through to the first half of 2018, my main objectives were to inform the world about the

12

ongoing genocide and to undertake humanitarian activities to support our people. I assisted the Department of Health and Social Services and coordinated the donation of over-the-counter medications to some of our refugees in neighboring Nigeria. I also reached out to my local churches, and they organized prayer sessions, which I believe to be important, as the power of prayer can never be taken for granted or undermined. I also reached out to political leaders like Congresswoman Karen Bass who had already made her voice heard on this crisis. It was no longer an internal socio-political problem; it was now becoming a concern for the international community. But what was the hold up? The situation clearly concerned two nations with distinct and unique colonial histories, which did not allow them to function as a single nation. One of those contacts was with the US Ambassador to LRC, Mr. Peter Barlerin. I wrote to him pleading for help for our people. Below is a copy of my email to Ambassador Barlerin and his response:

May 25, 2017 Email to Peter Barlerin, the U.S. Ambassador to Cameroon

His Excellency, the US Ambassador to Cameroon,

I am a U.S. citizen originally from Southern Cameroons. I want to thank you for acknowledging the current humanitarian crisis in the Southern Cameroons. I equally want to thank you for openly denouncing the government of LRC for the atrocities perpetuated on the people of Southern Cameroons.

As I write this email, there is a well-orchestrated genocide in my homeland. If the international powers of the world that are supposed to protect human rights and defend the weak and the poor do not step in now, the blood of these thousands of innocent victims will be on their heads.

You have been objective so far in your words. Now is the time for action against LRC. Please do something urgently.

Thank You!

-Patience Abiedu,

A very concerned U.S. citizen

Response from U.S. Ambassador Cameroon Barlerin, Peter H Sun, Jun 10, 2018

Thank you for writing, Ms. Abiedu, and apologies for not responding sooner. We have condemned violence on both sides while avoiding use of terms like "terrorist" or "genocide" and calling for meaningful dialogue that can be agreed to by both sides, as that is the essential meaning of dialogue. May you and your family remaining in Cameroon be kept safe from harm.

-Peter

His response gave me some hope that the international community was not oblivious to the unfolding tragedy in our homeland after all.

One beautiful Sunday morning, I received a phone call from one of my friends. She said, "Congratulations on your appointment." I had no idea what she was talking about, and after inquiring further, I learned that I had been called to serve in the Interim Government as the Deputy Chair of the Ethics Commission. My conviction to work towards restoring our independence was reaffirmed, and I have since then worked diligently within the different administrative structures of our movement, including our Local Government Areas (LGA). The LGA and County structures are fundamental in resource mobilization and utilization. The concept behind the slogan,

14

"defending one's county, LGA by LGA" is essentially the best recipe for achieving unity, because it would expedite the process of gaining complete independence for Ambazonia. Therefore, I strongly believe it is crucial for all Southern Cameroonians who support our struggle to commit to and actively participate in the activities of their Local Government Areas.

For years, the Biya regime made no efforts to engage in dialogue, preferring threats, edicts, and the pursuit of policies to subjugate our people by every means. How can we forget that even after Cameroonian Parliamentarian Honorable Joseph Wirba made his famous intervention in the Cameroonian parliament and reprimanded the Cameroonian government with the statement - "when injustice is law, resistance becomes a duty" no positive changes were made? Such a statement justified our struggle. He would later flee the country into exile because in La Republique du Cameroun, no one challenges Biya and lives to see another day. Unfortunately, Biya and his cohorts have ignored his warning.

Today, Ambazonians are resisting the occupier forces with sticks, traditional ceremonial guns, and now, smuggled AK47s or whatever they can capture from the invading BIRs, some of whom would rather go AWOL than be sent into our territory to fight. Our restoration fighters have, on various occasions, dealt severe blows to the BIR forces who often enter Ambazonian territory to commit arson, rape our girls, loot, and shoot any Ambazonian boy in sight.

Thus, the collective Anglophone distrust and anger towards BIR and the Biya administration is justified. Aside from the carnage, we have not forgotten the many names we have been called in order to denigrate and dehumanize us. We have been called Anglofools, "les Bamendas," Biafrans, "enemies in the house," dogs, and cockroaches, by Biya's administrators sent to rule over and subjugate us. We have been made to feel like second-class citizens on Southern Cameroonian soil. We are treated like prisoners of war on our own land.

If you are from the Southern Cameroons, kindly reflect on the following questions: How can we forget all the terrible things that have happened to our people? How can we forget the torture, incarceration, raping, maiming, burning, and execution of our sons and daughters? Who has not seen those painful videos of elderly grandparents in their twilight years, hiding in bushes because their homes have been burnt to ashes? Who has not seen those videos which show the burial of our loved ones killed by LRC's army?

How can we forget that after the peaceful protests by teachers and lawyers, there were no solutions to address their concerns? On the contrary, they were arrested and treated like common criminals. How can we forget the use of helicopter gunships to attack peaceful protesters, followed by mass arrests and incarcerations? How can we forget the prevalence of extra-judicial killings and the scorched-earth policy of LRC that has resulted in hundreds of villages destroyed?

How can we forget the BIR butchers or the LRC regional administrator ordering our people to evacuate their villages or face unimaginable consequences? Who suffers such indignities and remains unmoved? How can we forget that Southern Cameroons, a land of plenty, a land of picturesque beauty on the Gulf of Guinea, now lies derelict, destroyed by LRC? I say, "No! No! No!" We must never forget what Biya, and his Army of Occupation have done. We have been thrust into a war in which we must defend ourselves until we reach the promised land, if not for ourselves, for future generations.

It saddens me that most of the Francophone population could

not rise against Biya's regime in solidarity with Anglophones, whom they call brothers. This shows that our plight is not their fight. For this, current and future generations will never forget how our so-called brothers have coldly abandoned us to the macabre whims of their real brothers—the forces of French Cameroun.

You see, the French Cameroun system is defined by cronyism, dishonesty, corruption, nepotism, tribalism, and injustice. Everywhere, these social ills exist as a plague in some form or fashion. Some of these problems can be rectified by good governance. However, the issues facing Southern Cameroons are not ills that good governance can fix. We have an existential problem and a question of sovereignty. We will determine our degrees of vexations when we reach Buea. When we have our country back, we will fly our flag within the distinct and recognizable boundaries of our homeland.

Oh, we must never forget the elephant in the room —France. In the sixties, France began granting what it called independence to its colonies. In reality, it was just a charade. I call this 'pseudo-independence' because the reality is that policies were put in place to ensure that France remained firmly in control of the political, economic, and social aspects of life in their former colonies. The window-dressing is still being achieved today thanks to people like Biya who epitomize the diabolic neocolonialist French project in Africa. To maintain its grip, France has been complicit in the systematic subjugation of parts of Africa, resourcing and sustaining the likes of Biya to brutally quell dissent or alternative views, leading to murders, assassinations, disappearances, and so-called political imprisonment. As a 'reward' for supporting and sustaining dictators in their former colonies, France allegedly steals about 500 billion dollars annually from some African nations. To be really free,

Ambazonia must sever any umbilical connection with France through French Cameroun. Ambazonia must be free! We are a nation worth fighting for.

To ensure that we never forget, I envision a proper memorial in honor of all our fallen heroes, their names engraved in gold. It will be a permanent testament to their bravery and sacrifice of tears, sweat, and blood. It must tell the world and generations to come, the harrowing terror, suffered at the hands of a brutal dictator—Biya, and his yes-men. It will tell the story of a friendly, proud, defiant (but normally peaceful) and loving people thrust into war that they never wanted, expected, or prepared for. However, when a situation as devasting as this one arises, a people's only choice is to defend themselves and their homeland. No, we must never forget!

I find myself asking whether the international community is remotely relevant to our struggle for freedom. Many developed nations in the world have gone through periods of instability, social upheaval, depression, or war. Countries like Eritrea, Sudan, and Rwanda all have very dark periods in their histories. We are not an exception. Nonetheless, before the international powers intervene, if at all they would, we, Southern Cameroonians, must decide what we want and how to get it. We will not be manipulated by any leaders or organizations, including the United Nations or African Union. They cannot dictate what we ought to do to bring peace to our homeland. Our homeland is a part of Africa with internationally recognized boundaries. Within these boundaries reside a people, blessed with resources which they and only they have the right to tap and harness to develop and sustain their country the way they want to. My homeland is the greatest place on earth to call home. Therefore, we have every reason to preserve it and to protect the freedom to own it.

The time has come for the world to practice what it preaches, for the world's community of nations to rise as one and support Ambazonia. The world must stop France from its pillage and plunder of Africa. The days of colonialism and neo-colonialism in Southern Cameroons/Ambazonia are numbered. There has been untold suffering (physical, mental, and emotional); loss of lives in the most horrendous ways imaginable, and dispossession of people through the wanton destruction of the property built/developed/acquired through the sweat, hard work, and ingenuity of Southern Cameroonians. Therefore, the restoration of our statehood and independence is non-negotiable. But before the international powers of the world make any decision on the future of Southern Cameroons/Ambazonia, if they would, we Southern Cameroonians/Ambazonians must write our own story. We must decide on what ending we want to that story. It should be written across our foreheads in indelible ink that the only option for peace to reign is for LRC and the Southern Cameroons to exist as good neighbors.

I have been dreaming of a nation where our education is comparable to that in the great schools and universities in the Anglo Saxon heritage the world over; I dream of a legal system whose pillars are the best traditions of judicial independence and the rule of law; I dream of a first-class healthcare system; I dream of Ambazonia as an economic powerhouse whose blood and arteries are a 21st-century infrastructure and a booming economy that together support entrepreneurship; I dream about our great agricultural potential which will make our food self-sufficiency the envy of our soon-to-be neighbors and the world. Tell me then—Why would any bona fide Southern Cameroonian not yearn to celebrate a free Ambazonia?

I hope my journey from a 'Unitarist' to a 'Restorationist'

motivates Southern Cameroonians who are still sitting on the fence—to take a leap of faith and fight for the country we want. Ambazonia will be free through our combined efforts. Hail the land of glory; God, the watchman of our nation, is watching.

CHAPTER 2

TRYING TO MAKE SENSE OF IT ALL:

MY THOUGHTS & FEELINGS AS THE WAR PROGRESSES

DOROTHY NGWA

I remember always wishing that Cameroon never goes to war, especially after watching the horrors caused by wars in foreign countries always being displayed on television. I thought it would be impossible for a president to declare ware on' While our restoration forces, our young sons -some barely getting to the age of maturity - are now the ones defending our homeland with machetes and ceremonial guns that our forefathers used for rites of passage and burials, French Cameroun's killing machine (also known as the Rapid Intervention Brigade) has not let up its evil resolve to annihilate Southern Cameroonians.

In the past year, we have organized Ambazonia into Local Government Areas (LGAs), structures designed to coordinate our efforts for defending the homeland and self-help during this war which was imposed on us by the French Cameroun leadership. In a recent video of my village shared in my LGA WhatsApp group, I watched with disgust how it has now been transformed into mile after mile of destruction and devastation eerily compounded by it having been deserted by its inhabitants. Every house abandoned, markets deserted, schools burned down, and children's play areas enveloped by silence. The empty streets added to the specter of a "ghost" village, similar to hundreds of other villages across the Southern Cameroons, scorched by an evil government invaders and abandoned by the people who used to them home. Where once kings and queens ruled; where women birthed life, where men hunted, gathered, and cared for loving families, and protected kingdoms, artifacts, relics, and women fed and grew children, and enforced mores; all is desolate. In homesteads and communities along the main roads, the overgrown grass is taller than the houses which they surround, a poignant reminder of the long absence of their caretakers and owners who have been forced into 'exile' or the great beyond. Communities once full of life now lie in ruin, their inhabitants killed or forced to flee into the bush or to seek sanctuary elsewhere. I was forced to ask myself several questions. Where did we go wrong to deserve this? How do I make sense of all of this?

Why should Ambazonians be forced into a war for demanding their basic human rights to live freely in their God-given land? Are we not human beings and do we not deserve to live life with dignity? The inability to provide answers to these questions often makes me wonder why the world cannot see and understand that the fundamental human right we seek—to live in our land as an independent people—is so valid and legal that even a child could understand it. This makes the war imposed on us by Paul Biya's government blatantly obvious as a sinister campaign to dispossess us of our God-given inheritance and to consign us to perpetual subservience. I will therefore not stop wondering why such a terrible injustice has befallen us, or why the world sits still in a conspiracy of silence, seemingly paralyzed by conspiracy itself.

Despite our limitations and struggles, I thank God for America, my own safe haven. May God bless her for her spirit of hospitality and for giving me the chance to live a dignified life and feel like a human being. I encourage every Ambazonian in the diaspora to say a prayer of thanksgiving for their host country. One day, by the grace of God, the Federal Republic of Ambazonia (FRA) will also become a haven for other oppressed peoples who fear persecution and flee from dictators and murderous regimes.

Immeasurable thanks to Ambazonians in the diaspora for providing funds for projects and initiatives in our homeland. Their support has significantly kept up the defense of our homeland, making it ungovernable by the dictatorial regime of Paul Biya despite the large deployment of his troops in the Southern Cameroons to achieve his murderous goal of annihilating our people. Paul Biya's superior military power, bolstered by troops from some French-speaking African countries and the French army, and funded through diverted U.S. backed military assistance, is yet to defeat us and end our quest for the restoration of our independence. Paul Biya and his government have sought the assistance of other countries to arrest Ambazonian activists in the Diaspora as they did with the abduction and handing over of our leaders from the Nera hotel in Nigeria[2] to French Cameroun to face sham trials in military tribunals for what only they and their warped minds can define as treason and terrorism. But justice, good sense, and reason are on our side. I read a piece on social media in which an American envoy—Tibor Nagy, was asked why the U.S has not arrested Ambazonians in his country for encouraging our young men and boys to defend the homeland. He responded by saying, "If they are not breaking the laws of the United States, there is no reason to arrest them." This certainly was

---

[2] The Southern Cameroonian leaders who were kidnapped at Nigeria's Nera hotel are often referred to as the "Nera-10" and "Nera 37".

not the response LRC expected to hear from him.

Over the years, the calculated oppression of Ambazonians by French Cameroun has compelled many of us to leave our homeland in search of a better life elsewhere. A turning point has now been reached. In the past, the voices of Southern Cameroonian political exiles were largely lost or never heard in some cases. Today, the crescendo of the voices of millions of Southern Cameroonians now living in the Diaspora, who witness their families being slaughtered by French Cameroun forces, is growing louder in urgency and intensity as they call out the occupation and genocide in Ambazonia.

They are saying, "No" with their Euros, Dollars, Yens, and Pounds Sterling. For this reason, LRC, is even more furious. Instead of doing the right and just thing, Paul Biya has spared no effort in using the money earned from the resources from our dear homeland/territory to hire big lobby firms in every major capital city around the world in order to sell a false and self-serving narrative that terrorists and treasonous "Anglophones" were trying to destabilize and break up his "one and indivisible peaceful" country. We are unfazed by this. The truth always prevails over falsehood, the determination of this never-ending generation will settle for nothing less than independence for Ambazonia.

We are winning because the brave boys defending our homeland have refused to cede even an inch of our territory to Paul Biya's invading forces, and they are determined to never again submit to enslavement by French Cameroun. God has a way of turning the wickedness on the wicked back on them. Their sons in military uniforms sent to kill our children return to them in lifeless body bags. Out of shame, the actual number of such body bags returned to Paul Biya has never been fully counted nor revealed to the world. While our goal was never to be violent, we believe in protecting our own.

24

I am old enough to remember the days when West Cameroon and East Cameroon, two distinct states entered an ill-fated 'federation.' I also remember the period when our money changed from shillings to francs. At eight years old, I used to walk with friends from Clerk's Quarter, a neighborhood in Buea, to the orchards in Victoria, just to eat free fruit and walk back home happily, without being harassed by anyone. Those were the good old days. Yes, there was serenity, cleanliness, a true respect for humanity, and a cherished spirit of hospitality in West Cameroon.

Shortly after the completion of the currency change to the Communauté Financière d'Afrique Franc (CFA), things deteriorated fast; the nightmare for West Cameroonians had just begun. The name West Cameroon was abolished. This area, formerly an autonomous state that had enjoyed peace and proper democratic rule, was, without consultation of its custodians, suddenly broken up into two parts called the "Northwest and Southwest Provinces." A people and a territory once contiguous became Balkanized to achieve the evil goal of divide and rule. From that point onwards, oppression, dehumanization, and dispossession were unleashed upon us.

I lack the right words to describe the political relationship between English-speaking Cameroon and French-speaking Cameroon. Some people have described it as an "illegal union." For others, it is a "failed marriage" which quickly turned into a continuing nightmare for the Southern Cameroons, the English-Speaking part. Since Paul Biya declared war on the people of Ambazonia in 2017, the relationship has descended into a matter of life and death for Ambazonians—a new reality of escape and survival. This had been the case long before the declaration of war; the only difference is the scale of the brutality our people have experienced in the last three years, which has made its way into the chronicles of writers and organizations that care to report the atrocities, even if the world chooses to turn a blind eye.

I feel sad each time I think of the good old days of West Cameroon. Was paradise lost? I wonder why the two-state federation was abolished. In my opinion, it was not the best option, but our parents had taken us down that path all the same, and some of them were determined to make it work. I try to make sense of it all. In my wondering, I have looked at Canada, where Anglophones and Francophones live cordially and peacefully within a defined constitutional arrangement. I often wonder why we could not replicate that.

I ache at the thought that Ambazonians must put up with the revolting knowledge that we are orphans, treated like a conquered people by the people of French Cameroon at the behest of France. I am convinced that Cameroonian Francophones and Anglophones are naturally incompatible. Our values/way of life are markedly different. To have been yoked into a nightmarish relationship with French Cameroon for fifty-seven years, in which we have wanted out for the most part of that time, is hellish. This makes separation between Southern Cameroons and French Cameroon the only sensible and moral solution to prevent the extinction of the Ambazonian as a species on planet earth. Our independence is no longer up for discussion, negotiation, or any such time-waster.

October 1, 2017, was the darkest day of my life in this revolution. I saw images of human intestines gushing out of the lifeless bodies of unarmed Southern Cameroonian civilians of all ages. They had been brutally murdered by the blood-thirsty and trigger-happy invading forces of French Cameroon on the ground and from the air in a helicopter gunship. Our people had truly found their voices to declare and celebrate the restoration of our independence. But this dream was momentarily disturbed by the guns and thuggish soldiers dispatched by Paul Biya to silence the sounds of freedom. I asked myself why anyone would need helicopters or guns and live ammunition to control chanting and placard-bearing peaceful protesters. I am still trying to make sense of the terrible events and haunting images of that day. I wept. I still weep. On some days, I cannot find sleep. I am still horrified by the carnage of one of the most important of days to Southern Cameroonians. I naively thought that the United Nations, the African Union, or the international community would be so outraged to the point of stepping in to stop the killings and resolve this most important of matters to Southern Cameroonians.

Well, it has been more than three years of unending massacres, burning down of houses and whole villages, lynching and maiming, and the callous disregard for human suffering. My heart still bleeds when I remember those horrifying images of the toddler who was callously thrown into boiling palm oil by the soldiers of French Cameroon. This is one of many dastardly and macabre actions of Francophone soldiers that defy reason and conscience. I wonder how that toddler, who had been abandoned by her fleeing mother, could be a terrorist by any stretch of imagination. But the testament here is that no one, not even the innocent, are spared in Paul Biya's murderous onslaught.

I freak out as the death toll rises from hundreds to thousands. I am helpless as our villages are burnt to the ground—hundreds of them. I am perplexed by how French Cameroon can consistently defy all international norms, laws, and conventions in the face of a seeming global and collective helplessness. I am just trying to make sense of it all. I know I am not alone in this quest to reclaim our freedom and independence mentally and physically—Ambazonia calls.

Our interim President, during his 2017 visit to the United States, said that if God wanted us to be Americans, then he would have caused us to be born in America. This statement is so true. God does not make mistakes. He caused us to be born to Ambazonian parents for a reason. On the day of reckoning, He will ask you, "I sent you to Ambazonia. What difference did you make there in my name?" What will you say? I am pleading to my fellow Ambazonians both at home and abroad, who can do something, to come to the aid of our suffering families. They should join as one to liberate our homeland.

I am humbled to be able to freely express my thoughts and feelings about this revolution through this book. As disappointed as I am, I believe there is still hope for the future, not only for Ambazonians but also for all oppressed people everywhere in the world. The world can be a better place; we just need to be deliberate and selfless in our acts of love, unendingly questing for a just peace. I believe that my shattered faith in the United Nations will be restored when they reconsider and take the right actions to end the war and act for justice for Ambazonia. My voice is just one of the millions of Ambazonian voices crying out for justice, peace, freedom, and a better future for our children. I plead with the international community, especially with the Secretary-General of the United Nations, Anthony Guiterres to reconsider and reinstate Mathew Lee, the journalist who for about a year now, has suffered because he speaks the truth to those in power. The UN must play its part in Ambazonia, as it does in other parts of the world, to resolve the conflict and bring about a permanent peace.

My Advice to Ambazonian Children:

To our children, who are our future, as you fashion the future

28

now, I leave you with these words of the apostle Paul in Philippians 4:8-9: "Finally, brothers, whatever is true, whatever is honorable, whatever is just, whatever is pure, whatever is commendable, if there is any excellence, if there is anything worthy of praise, think about these things. What you have learned and received and heard and seen in me, practice these things and the God of peace will be with you."

CHAPTER 3

HOW AND WHY I GOT INVOLVED IN THE STRUGGLE

MARTHA SHEY

It all started at 9:00 am on a Monday in February 2017. I received a call from a professor, who we will call Mr. X. "Good morning Mrs. Shey. Where are you? Why are you not in class? You were supposed to have a lesson with your level two students from 8:00 am to noon," Mr. X ranted on the phone. I felt compelled to answer.

I politely greeted him. "Professor, today is Monday—you know, it is 'Ghost Town.' There are no taxis in the streets. There is no way I can get to Bambili. Professor, remember that my car was vandalized during the strike two weeks ago?" I replied. But my explanation did not mean much to him.

"Taxi services were running from six o'clock this morning," the Professor shot back. "Why didn't you leave at that time? This is the third time I am talking to you about your absence from class," he added. I braced myself for the warning. "The Minister has said even if there is just one student in class, you must go ahead with your lesson and teach. I must remind you that the children of Captain Yves, the Brigade Commander for the military, were in class today while you were absent. He has just called threatening to call the

30

Governor of the Northwest Region about government teachers not showing up for work," he continued, his voice desperate. "You people don't understand the difficulties I face with the Minister of Education. The next time you are absent from your lecture on account of the Ghost Town, I will give your number to him so you can explain why you are not in class teaching your students and answer his queries directly," he finished and hung up the phone. I was expecting that call, as it had become a recurrent event for me over the past three weeks. As I placed my phone down on my table, I wished I could tell him to go to hell. Who did he want to kill just so a certain brigade commander's child would be taught a lesson? What about the thousands of children who were unable to be chauffeur-driven in army cars to school? Yes, we had officially entered into the resistance phase of the war declared by Paul Biya in our country which French Cameroun calls Northwest and Southwest Regions. I was living the war, wondering what would become of us.

The previous Monday morning, after receiving the now-familiar call to defy the Ghost Town and to risk my life, I managed to get into the lecture room around 11:30 a.m., where I found ten students out of a total of 120, all of them from French Cameroun, waiting for the lecture. Not wanting to be seen as a stubborn colleague who did not care about the pressure on the Vice Chancellor of the University from the Minister of Higher Education, I reluctantly entered the lecture room. I was irked by the cunning smiles on the students' faces telling me that they had won. Notwithstanding this, I vowed to continue the resistance in millions of other ways against French Cameroun, including civil disobedience. Therefore, after nearly two hours of endless blah-blah-Blah 'teaching,' I left the lecture room with the intention of going to the office to do some administrative work. Instead, I walked to my car, opened the door, and slumped behind the wheel, downcast, fearful, tearful, and tense. The atmosphere around me was ominous. There was little or no life for miles and miles in a once-bustling hub of activity because of the Ghost Town edict. Then, my phone rang. A voice came on — "Ms. Shey?"

"Yes", I replied and then asked, "who is this?"

The voice was strange and unfamiliar. Then the caller continued, speaking in Cameroonian Pidgin English:

"We know say you be hold class today wey na ghost town day. How manage you Anglophone person you go for class weh ya own people di suffer?" the unidentified caller asked. I could not answer.

(Translation: We know you held class today when it's a ghost town day. How could you, an Anglophone hold class when your own people are suffering?)

"Na wuna di spoil this thing enh? We know ya motor and even the place wey you di stay."

My grip on the phone became tighter, frozen with fear that I had done the unthinkable to incur the wrath of my own people by lacking the backbone to stay away from lectures. Fear and shame enveloped me in an instant. I tried not to run. The caller continued:

"Next time wey you no respect ghost town[3], we go visit you. We dey warn you. We know all ting wey e di pass for campus."

He then hung up the phone. Hanging up was a relief of sorts because I had nothing to say in reply. I was in the proverbial rock

---

[3] Ghost Town: A day long curfew mandated by the Southern Cameroonian soldiers in order to rebel and resist against the Cameroonian Government.

and a hard place—the government would sack me for not teaching; however, if I taught, I would be defying the ghost town imposed by the restoration forces. I was too scared to drive alone back home. So, I called a friend who was also on campus, and we drove home together.

After that episode, I wrestled with many existential questions. Did I have rights? Why the blatant disregard for the voices and wellbeing of Ambazonians? Why are Ambazonians second-class citizens in their own homeland? Who decreed this? Were we in a military state? Will this ever end? How? What will happen to us as a people? What will happen to our homeland? Is this what our founding fathers signed up for when they faithfully joined French Cameroun in 1961? I have been waking up to these questions. My distress at living our nightmare every day, every hour, has only increased. So, when I again received another call from the Vice Chancellor on the same day, I struggle to remember what I said to him. It was the beginning of the end. When the call ended, I screamed to myself, saying, "Martha, you've had enough of this. This situation has to change. We cannot let future generations of Ambazonians endure this mess, this stress." I found my resolve.

It was then that I decided to become actively involved in the struggle for change. Going back to the beginning. After completing my university studies in Yaoundé, the capital city of French Cameroun in the late 80s, all my attempts at scoring a job were futile. I wrote three competitive exams to join the civil service. I succeeded in the written part but never made it through the oral part of these tests. The system was rigged in favor of Francophone candidates. Southern Cameroonians had somehow been blacklisted.

The worst of my experiences was in 1991. I had succeeded in passing the written part of the exams into the Cameroon School of

Magistracy (ENAM)—Cycle A. But I had already left for Europe a month earlier. However, I decided to go back to Cameroon for the oral examinations. I was carrying a parcel for one of my former lecturers, whose sister I had met in Europe. When I went to his office to deliver the parcel, he asked the reason for my return to Cameroon after the golden opportunity of being in Europe. I told him that I came back to take my orals for entrance into ENAM. To my surprise, he told me that he had the list of admitted candidates—but my name wasn't on it. Mind you, I'd returned a week before the orals were to take place. He then pulled the list from his drawer and showed it to me, explaining that the list had been sent to him from the Presidency. I murmured, "How can that be?" I then reminded myself that in Cameroon, that was the norm. It dawned on me that like in George Orwell's Animal Farm, some Cameroonians were deemed more important than others.

After 27 years of a successful life in Europe (educationally, professionally, and family-wise), and even though I felt I owed Cameroon nothing, the love for my homeland pushed me to accept a teaching position at the University of Bamenda in 2014. I decided to go back 'home' and contribute to our nation-building efforts. However, shortly after settling down to my teaching position, I began to observe the "Francophonization" of the educational system, and how it made things difficult for children from English-speaking regions to make their way through the system. Another shocking thing I observed was how people were appointed to lead positions not based on merit, but as compensation for their political appurtenance and their Francophone background. For example, posts of directors were reserved for Francophones and preferably those who were in the ruling political party, the Cameroon People's Democratic Movement.

Few Anglophones could only dream of being assistant directors. I can recall when a Francophone agronomist was preferred to be the head of a School of Transport and Logistics—a field which he was not knowledgeable about at all. This same Director would rather use his Francophone brothers (who themselves were not in the field) to set and grade competitive entrance examinations and other activities, than engage the services of qualified professionals of Southern Cameroonian (Anglophone) origin.

In the several professional schools that make up the University of Bamenda (UBA), the staff is predominantly French-speaking (not even bilingual), and they had to teach technical courses in French at an English-speaking university – located in an English-speaking city. When students complained and pointed out that UBA is an English-speaking University with English being the main language of instruction, they were bluntly told that they had no choice but to deal with their courses being instructed in French. The Francophone director of my school went as far as saying that it was a favor that the Southern Cameroons students were being taught in French, after all, they reminded the students, all the companies that would eventually employ them are found in French-speaking Cameroon. The student body too was highly becoming Francophone and it was very common to hear the French language everywhere on campus, not because of the bilingual nature of the institution, but because the number of Francophone students was on a continuous rise. This brought back very bad memories of my own university days at the Ngoa-Ekélé campus when we Southern Cameroonians had to spend all our weekends trying to translate lectures from French to English. One could sense the mounting tension in and around campus, as it was obvious that things were not going well.

Not long after, the outburst from the lawyers' strike was

followed by the teachers' strike. After the arrest of the SCACUF leaders (including Balla and Fontem), the university lecturers under the teachers' union decided to stay away from classes in support of their colleagues. The Francophone lecturers (thanks to their high numbers) threatened the Anglophone lecturers, defied the strike, and wrote a letter to the Minister of Higher Education, denouncing the Vice Chancellor for instigating the strike and hatred for Francophones. The result was an atmosphere of suspicion since Francophone and Anglophone colleagues could no longer interact freely. With the advent of ghost towns, many students and lecturers showed their support for the struggle by staying away from the campus on Mondays, except those of French-speaking origin.

The Minister of Higher Education, in support of the Francophones students, decreed that class must go on, even if there would be only one student in the class. Teachers who respected the ghost town and did not attend class would be summoned by the Governor and threatened with the risk of losing their salaries and outright dismissal. That is how each time an Anglophone lecturer stayed away from class, the few Francophone students, who defied the strike, would hurriedly draw report to the authorities. After I was threatened three times, I told myself that what I thought was a mistake was a well-calculated act of annexation by the government. Then I began to recall memories of my childhood under the federal system.

My Most Painful Moments in the Struggle

Despite my decision to join the change process, I had thought that it was right to add my voice to the voices of others and make the cry louder for the powers that be to hear us. My wish was that the Yaoundé authorities would lend an ear to the demands of the Anglophones and to right the wrongs. I kept comparing Cameroon to a polygamous family in which one of the wives and her children are unhappy with the treatment their husband and father was giving them. I kept hoping that one day Yaoundé would realize that things have been on a decline for a long time and that the curve needed to be reversed. The most I ever thought of was a return to the federal system, where we could manage our affairs as it used to be in the 60s when I was a child. However, my hopes were dashed when the Yaoundé regime, rather than listen to the cries of the people, decided to inflict more pain both verbally and through military action. To hear an administrator call us 'dogs' was so painful but witnessing them treating us like game that one shoots at a hunting range hurt and horrified me even more.

September 22, 2017, will remain one of my darkest days in this revolution. It was a moment when we flooded the roads with 'peace plants,' symbolizing a peaceful demonstration, but we were sprayed with bullets, even from helicopters. Then I understood again that everything being done against the people of the Southern Cameroons was a well-calculated plan of action, and that I needed to wake up from my daydream.

Another painful moment in this struggle was the 5th of January 2018 when our leaders were abducted from the Nera Hotel in Abuja, Nigeria and deported to LRC to stand trial for fictitious charges of treason, terrorism, and more. I had never felt this pain in my entire life. My stomach churned. My eyes could not close no matter how much I tried to close them. I lay in my bed watching the ceiling all night.

I felt like crying, but no sound could emerge from my voice. I felt like thorns were stabbing my heart. I wished I could melt like ice so as not to face that hurtful reality, but there was no way out. I literally fell sick and had to take a week of sick leave from my job.

My world had come to an end. Other painful moments are the images of the LRC forces burning homes and entire villages. The images of Mami Appi and many others burnt in their homes made me weep profusely. I can't imagine how a human being can do this to another human being. Most people don't live in huts by choice. That's all they have. When you burn their huts, how do you expect them to survive? The atrocities committed in the Southern Cameroons by the Yaoundé regime have made me think that they are deprived of all human sentiments—love, fear, shame, pity. I have therefore moved from a Federalist to a supporter of independence because I truly believe that we, Southern Cameroonians, and the people from French Cameroun are not meant to stay together.

My Proudest Moments in this Struggle

Despite the profusion of tears that I have shed since this struggle began, I nonetheless had some proud moments, the kind that put a smile on one's face. These were the kinds of moments that brought back the pride of being a Southern Cameroonian and reassured me that we were on the right track. The Honorable Joseph Wirba delivered a landmark speech at the LRC National Assembly. At last, I felt, somebody was bold enough to tell LRC to their faces that enough was enough. My pride was even greater in the light of the fact that I know Hon. Wirba personally, as we attended school together. I was proud to see that the integrity he showed as a student had grown to make him the people's voice.

Today, many months have gone by, and my pride has even grown deeper because his speech is turning out to be prophetic. The Southern Cameroons is actually bringing down LRC, as the latter's economy has taken a turn for the worse. Another such moment was the October 1, 2018 celebrations in Boyo County in the Northern Zone. This was the celebration of the first anniversary of the restoration of our independence. Despite the tight security, our people still showed up in grand style on this day. Videos of their celebration brought tears of joy to my eyes.

This brought back memories of my childhood when we used to celebrate "Empire Day." It was a clear indication that our people were determined to gain their independence at any cost. The ten-day lock-down of February 2019 (and the Ghost Town) are always proud moments for me because they show LRC, in particular, and the world at large, that Ambazonians are the ones ruling Ambazonia. They pay the piper and also call the tune.

Why an Independent Ambazonia is the Only Way Forward

One very good thing that the revolution has done on an international level is to force the world to know more about the history of Cameroon. I, like many other Southern Cameroonians born in the sixties, had been wondering what happened to our corporations such as the Public Works Department (PWD), Yoké Hydro Electric, Cameroon Bank, and Tole Tea that were the economic backbone of the Southern Cameroons? Today, it is crystal clear that the gradual deterioration of the situation and the erosion of our Anglo-Saxon values by the Yaoundé regime was not an error, but a well-planned act. And to make things worse, rather than pretending or even trying to right the wrongs, they have arrogantly decided to physically exterminate us. Proof of this arrogance is demonstrated, among other ways, by the responses given when some of our brave representatives tried to draw the attention of the Yaoundé regime to our plight.

At the beginning of the struggle, the rogue regime in Yaoundé did all it could to deceive its surrogates that "Cameroon was one and indivisible." But Ambazonians, in their resolve, have constantly and steadily stated historical facts that prove the contrary. Today the 'one and indivisible' slogan has gradually given way to a new slogan of 'living together' (le vivre ensemble). The question now is how do we continue to live together after all the atrocities inflicted on our people? We have paid too high a price to settle for anything less than an independent Ambazonia. The ultimate sacrifice (bloodshed) has been made to redeem our land. Let the blood of our fallen heroes not go in vain.

The Role of the International Community

The role of the international community, as far as the struggle is concerned, cannot be overstated. If the UN and Britain had properly finalized the decolonization process back in the 60s, we would not be where we are today. They need to step in and right the wrongs that they caused in our homeland.

Diplomacy is often done behind closed doors, and it often takes time, as it involves a lot of actors and factors. This sometimes gives the impression that nothing is being done or that no one cares about our plight. However, one expects that international organizations should be more responsive, especially after the "Never Again" declaration following the Rwanda genocide of the 1990s.

CHAPTER 4

FROM DESOLATION TO VICTORY – A CRY FROM AMBAZONIA

MA ELI JAMBELELE

The tide has arisen!

A mighty wave has broken off the shore

to engulf the Southern Cameroons like a tsunami!

I hear the wind

coming from the four corners

of Southern Cameroons,

Ambazonia

I see the Harmattan

That hot gale,

rushing down

from the Northern Zone

clad in red-hot hue.

It blows, it puffs, it blusters

— and the cry is:

"Freedom or death to the last man standing!"

Killings, torture chambers,

arbitrary arrests, human rights violations

of all forms and shapes

have failed to stem the tide

of Ambazonian resistance

The reign of terror and suppression,

mass distribution of public funds

To divide and confuse the Ambazonian people

have all woefully failed.

Yes, Ambazonians have sprung to life

To shake off the fifty-eight-year yoke of slavery

To smash the greed of France

and its puppet—Paul Biya

That rogue president, who—

with no knowledge of English

Pretends to rule an English-speaking people

No, Biya has not understood

 a word by Southern Cameroons

for 58 years. For Biya,

Federation means "Assimilation"

plus "Special Status" to hide the flaws,

while destruction and murder rage on.

Yeah, see how great Biya's love

for personal gain is!

But greater still is his lack of love

for those he called kin.

Their death is his victory!

And to France he hands over the trophies

Stripped to the bone, the wealth of Ambazonia

– gold, silver, oil, timber, minerals

of all sorts and food of every kind—

is poured upon the laps of France.

which feeds fat on the yoke of slavery,

imposed on a defenseless people!

Chai!

Biya has also mastered a French recipe

for quelling the Ambazonian cry.

A cry for justice and independence.

He commands his soldiers:

"Crush them! Spray them with

bullets from helicopters!

Shoot! Kill! Burn them!"

And their homes in the bargain

Until they are forced into submission.

Then, you can teach the mangled,

the strangled and subdued the language of peace!

Watch out!

France has printed new Bibles too,

Ostensibly carried by its envoys

to a tortured people.

Yet, France is dismayed

that there arises from the tired embers of Africa,

an anti-France movement!

Ah, France has robbed Africa of its very life!

But Biya is the Puppet

The Enabler. The Killer!

He has set fire on our people!

Their corpses lie littered

like hard coal on the ground.

Thousands have fled to the bushes,

pursued by Biya's military,

Plagued by mosquitoes and snakes

Others have fled to the suburbs of Nigeria

And live in squalid, people-trafficker's dens.

Our wounded litter the forests…

They share their space with weeping

 children, hungry, cold, and desolate –

medicines and medical services in scant supply.

Ah!

Our young men

are hunted like partridges—-

slaughtered like cattle.

Our women are stripped of every vestige of dignity.

Raped and slaughtered and dumped!

Families are torn apart

Babies at the breast and pregnant women

Shot, quartered, decapitated!

Their corpses lie in the open

where flies gather in their millions.

Some are dumped in shallow holes —

or graves, as La Republic du Cameroun calls them... There is sorrow and consternation!

The only sound of joy in many abandoned villages,

Emanates from La Republique's military,

Gloating over their spoil — the Ambazonian dead!

Oh! My land groans!

My Country weeps!

Ambazonia stands dismayed

at the world's collective silence,

as it gazes on our distress with apathy.

Their cold unconcerned reply is,

"It is so everywhere, isn't it?"

But my people drop down by

their thousands and die from sheer fatigue.

Alas! They can cry no more.

Is the United Nations,

a living organ or a dead assembly?

Does the Commonwealth only

care for its grip on African riches?

With no concern for the African people

An ineffective organization—his

 and all those that hanker for money

are still devoid of every sentiment of justice.

Ah! Christian world, this is your doing.

Where is your message of love and

justice on which your laws are based?

Stand, aghast! For Greed has consumed

the Word you proclaim.

Be appalled!

But the story does not end here.

Ambazonians have stood up

for their freedom,

No more, will their heads

be bowed to imposters,

No more, will their land be

stripped to feed the thieves…

No more, will their children

be treated like trash!

No more will the elderly

 see their sacred sanctuary

reduced to Rubble.

Freedom or resistance

till the last man standing!

CHAPTER 5

NO ONE SHOULD EVER TAKE AWAY YOUR IDENTITY

MA MADO

The teachers' and lawyers' protests that took place in November 2016 opened my eyes to a new and painful reality as I witnessed the tyrannical regime of La Republic du Cameroun (LRC) exercise brutality and insanity on the people of the Southern Cameroons. The inhumane treatment of university students during a peaceful protest in Buea further precipitated my decision to join the struggle for the independence of the Southern Cameroons. I saw how young boys were mercilessly beaten and killed by LRC soldiers. These boys were forced to carry cement blocks and or heavy stones while being beaten at the same time by soldiers. Some were tied to poles before being beaten. Others were simply executed. The 'lucky' ones, if one could describe them as such, were abducted and ferried away to the notorious Kondengui Prison. Not even one of them was charged with a crime. Today they face LRC's military tribunals for fabricated and senseless crimes of secession and terrorism.

LRC soldiers broke into student rooms, dragged them out into standing muddy water, and told them to roll in it. Young girls were beaten bloody on their buttocks with sticks while others were raped. Some died during the beatings, others died later in the hospital from their injuries. Many have become disabled and most sustained long-lasting injuries.

As a woman and mother, the thought of continuous inhumane treatment of innocent children and the people of the Southern Cameroons makes my heart bleed. Tears still roll from my eyes every time I watch the horrible videos circulating on social media. Other times, watching these horrible pictures proved to be very difficult. One video in particular pushed me into joining this struggle.

I awoke one morning and decided to go through my phone as usual. I was not prepared for the shock I had watching a video of women weeping and rolling on the ground, mourning the loss of their children. The shouts and cries of a particular woman drove me to tears. She repeatedly called out in her lamentation, "Ricobel eh, where is Ricobel? He was among those arrested last. He was only 16 years of age and did not take part in any protest. Where have you put my son? Where did he go wrong? I need my child! Please bring back my son!" she wailed. As a mother, listening to these painful words and seeing the anguish on her face, I could not hold back my own tears.

It was later explained that soldiers arrested some innocent children and took them away. Their whereabouts were unknown. Later, the soldiers brought back only a few of the children after continuous rioting by the town's people. That they could not provide any information about the missing children nor say what had happened to them exponentially increased the heartbreak of families. It was then that I put myself in the place of those mothers who feared the worst for their children.

That was the moment I decided to do something to make the voices of our people heard. I created the Freedom Fighter Women's

Forum on WhatsApp. That gave birth to our first-ever demonstration which took place in Dusseldorf, Germany. This was later followed by the first-ever Southern Cameroon Women's Conference held in Essen, Germany a few weeks later. This was done in collaboration with other Ambazonian women.

One of my proudest moments in this struggle was the worldwide Southern Cameroon Million Women's March that took place on September 22, 2017, followed a few weeks later by the October 1st Restoration Worldwide Demonstration. Sadly, it ended up with many casualties and the loss of lives of our people killed by the armed forces of LRC.

The official declaration of war on our people in 2017 by the tyrannical regime of LRC permanently broke my heart. The rampant killing of our children, parents, and grandparents and the burning of houses and villages by LRC soldiers makes me sick. The in-house fighting amongst our people (everybody wanting to be a leader in this struggle) also drives me nuts. If I had the power, I would put an end to this on-going crisis. Every day before I go to bed, I pray and hope for a better tomorrow for the people of the Southern Cameroons. I wish that all that has happened will just be a nightmare.

To the future generations of the Southern Cameroons, I remind you that the people of the Southern Cameroons are one people. Our true story has been hidden from us from generation to generation. We were never taught our true history in school; we are treated like low-class citizens and not given the opportunity to excel. Any attempt to educate us about who we really are, is usually thwarted. Despite all the torments and pains being inflicted on our people, FREEDOM is what we should negotiate for. To you, the future generations of the Southern Cameroons, everything you are and what you stand for will always be your identity. Let nobody take that away from you. We shall overcome one day.

Long live the people of the Southern Cameroons and short live the struggle. God bless our young nation!

CHAPTER 6

WHY I JOINED THE AMBAZONIAN RESTORATION MOVEMENT

IRENE EMBELI NGWA

The consortium of Barrister Agbor Balla and Dr. Neba Fontem, a conglomerate of civil society organizations made up of mostly moderates and later dubbed the Federalist Front, was born in 2016 after all attempts by the civil society to collaborate with Paul Biya's Government to maintain our Anglo-Saxon education and legal systems failed. It is painful to dwell on reminders that our legal and education systems in the former British Southern Cameroons had been systematically degraded under colonialism/annexation by French Cameroun for nearly six decades. That same year, I visited Cameroon for my father's funeral. The indignities, economic degradation, political injustices, and miscarriages of justice at every level had escalated to alarming rates, leaving the people of my homeland hopeless and helpless.

As I pen these cold and painful lines, more than 3,000 of our civilian brothers, children, and sisters have been butchered within the past two years. The Consortium proposed an inclusive dialogue to fix our educational and legal systems within the Cameroon we used to know. This proposition was deemed to be a sustainable way to resolving what came to be known as the "Anglophone Problem," with the hope of fostering togetherness. But it was met with brutality from LRC. The Consortium were despised, tortured, arrested, and threatened with treasonous charges by the colonial regime in Yaoundé, and locked up in jail. This influenced the current the Southern Cameroons' liberation movement that has emerged locally and globally to fight La Republic du Cameroun.

The uniqueness of this liberation movement, which in a more concise rendition, has been tagged The Independence Movement for the Restoration of the Southern Cameroons, has, in less than three years, increased awareness about the political origins of the people of the former British Southern Cameroons, now called Ambazonia. The Consortium also helped to foist the plight of the people of Ambazonia on international consciences and consciousness.

It has inspired many Southern Cameroonians to be committed to forging a better place for the next generation. With the revelations of the misconduct that occurred during the 1961 plebiscite, the 1972 staged referendum; the 'Oui' and 'Yes' treachery at the ballot box, and the 1984 dissolution of the illegal federation and the automatic secession by LRC from the federation, this generation of Ambazonians are even more determined to stand up to the challenge of reclaiming their stolen statehood and re-building their own precious nation. The wanton human-rights abuses, which our people have experienced, have only intensified our resolve to reclaim our lost sovereignty. The question that should be asked is, "How and why did Irene Embeli Ngwa get so actively involved in the struggle?"

Before I attempt to present an outline of the reasons that led to my unapologetic involvement in the independence restoration of the nation where I was born and raised, permit me to explain my experiences with French Cameroun's master plan to completely obliterate our existence. As a teen, I lived in Yaoundé with my uncle, Chief Paul Agwenjang, who died fighting for the Social Democratic

Front (SDF) of Ni John Fru Ndi. I witnessed firsthand the discrimination against minority English-speaking Southern Cameroonians who were forced to travel hundreds of miles from the Southern Cameroons to Yaoundé in search of education and/or employment, or merely to perform a very mundane ritual—to certify state documents to get paid or to receive very slight administrative services. Yes, all that journey just for that. During my stay in Yaoundé, I became not just a French speaker but also a teacher. In 1987, only two years after I left Cameroon for the USA, I returned to Cameroon, and there, in a taxi, was Philip, my Southern Cameroonian brother, imposing French on me. Even though I quickly reacted by introducing myself to him, I could understand he had just graduated from a police college. Philip, like most others who happened to have been trained in the French system in Cameroun, behaved the same way, displaying this silly notion that French was somehow superior; fueling an attitude in them where they would not speak English even to their 'Anglophone' brothers.

Over the years, the people of the Southern Cameroons have seen their institutions, way of life-cultures, and ultimately, their dignity systematically undermined by LRC policies and practices. LRC's intentions from the illegal Federation of 1961, was to assimilate, annex, and keep us a conquered and enslaved people forever. We have seen French Cameroun and its scheming cohorts masterminding a distortion of historical records. It is a deliberate policy of French Cameroon to subject the people of the Southern Cameroons to slavery. For nearly six decades, we have known nothing but impunity, arrogance, exploitation, and marginalization. To make things worse, French Cameroun's reaction towards a genuine and peaceful request for basic governance changes in the Southern Cameroons has been met with disdain and disregard for basic human aspirations and things that make for a dignified life.

When I went home in 2016 for my father's burial, I was shocked that Victoria (now called Limbe), a Southern Cameroons city, had transformed into Francophone place. There was little or nothing to suggest that I was in a key Southern Cameroons city; I strained to catch even the slightest echoes of English—our language of commerce and education.

As a humanitarian, I have always had concerns about government policies and their consequences on people. Watching the increased senseless killings, maiming, rapes, and discrimination, I thought it was time for me to take a stand. As a solution-oriented person, I thought the best way to help was to stand up to the onslaught and to be a part of the inevitable change that beckoned. As a mother, I always want my daughters to confront challenges in spite of the difficulties involved. I believe in leading by example. I thought it would be a great thing to inspire them by my actions as a freedom fighter for our people in Ambazonia.

Many Ambazonians, including myself, have sought refuge in different nations around the world, but we still feel like second-class citizens, and therefore, need a place we can call home. I thought it would not be honorable to just sit and wait for others to fight and die for a free homeland, or just wait for that day when we, as a people return home, free from the clutches of LRC. However, I want to be a practical activist in the independence movement, to craft a new nation.

My unwavering involvement in this struggle is based on the precept that, after watching our people being humiliated and slaughtered like cattle every day, after hearing them cry for help, and watching as they are hauled like cattle to jails in distant places in LRC, it is incumbent that the main actors of this freedom struggle find common ground; on it, they can consistently reform, reinforce, and re-strategize as the revolution evolves so as to shorten the time for us to arrive and repossess Buea—our beautiful capital city. It is in the culture of our great people of Ambaland to be organized, especially at this time when we confront the cruelty of LRC. Our impact will be even greater when we set aside our personal egos to pursue common goals, and when the battle is won, to share a common inheritance.

My hope is that we do not allow our individual dreams to become bigger than the Ambazonian dream. Dialogue is an integral aspect of the Anglo-Saxon culture that we need to practice as we forge ahead with this struggle. In the end, we can win sooner, even as we overcome the hate, envy, and malice, ushered in by much infighting. For these beliefs, I have pledged my life to ensure freedom for my native land, Ambazonia.

CHAPTER 7

BRAVE, BATTERED AMBAZONIA: RECOVERING ITS SHATTERED HISTORY

DELAVIL LEKUNZE

Ambazonians are forced to defend their homeland. They are fighting because the international structures set up to stop the escalation of the genocide from ravishing them have failed to adequately respond to the situation. Despite numerous calls to world bodies to intervene, and despite numerous reports sent to leading institutions about the carnage in the Southern Cameroons (SC), very little effort has been made to address this worsening crisis. It is this neglect, especially by the United Nations, and the continued killings by La Republique du Cameroun (LRC) that fired up the people's determination to restore the shattered statehood of the nation of the Southern Cameroons. Unlike many years back, Ambazonians are no longer afraid to say: "Ambazonia must be free," "Ambazonia rising to fall no more," and "Aluta continua"—the fight continues; victory is certain.

The profound pain has turned many Amba women like me into Takembeng, a group of dedicated Ambazonian revolutionary women who come out only in very grave and dire circumstances to confront the danger and heartbreak that lurks and raise the awareness that only their sacred bodies can do. Takembengs' appearances are purposefully rare. They are often draped only in the barest minimum of clothing; their majestic and solemn appearance is made more poignant by the heartbreaking tears they shed and their wailing; all meant to shock the senses of even the hard-hearted to the awareness that their children, their families, and villages are in pain and under attack, and that the perpetrators must be dealt with.

The outing of the Takembengs on Sept 22, 2017, was the most memorable; many of them gathered overseas and outside their villages back at home that day of restoration of SC's independence. When they come out, it is a warning that they should never be taken lightly by those who know their power. As a Takembeng, how could I or anyone stay quiet as the blood of innocent children ran through our streets and farms? How could women, huddled in their forest hideouts in as they run from the dreaded LRC soldiers, survive childbirth? How could I stand by and watch as the army of La Republique du Cameroun burned our families in their homes? How can women be silent after Mami Api, a grandmother of over 80 years and others, too old to escape into the bushes, are burnt alive in their homes by LRC arsonist soldiers? Takembengs came out and I woke up to speak for them so that the slain do not die in vain and so that they can have justice.

Takembeng cries out and fights to stop the killing of our people. How could I be a mere observer, seeing that little boy in Kumbo, shot in the face at close range by BIR? Images on social media showing how the boy knelt down and begged to do a last prayer before dying are haunting. When he finished his prayer, the army officer took his money and still shot him dead. How can I remain silent while men of God are executed; the Ghanaian Pastor Isaac Attoh, Cameroonian Priest Alexander Sob, American Pastor Charles Wiesco Truman, Kenyan Rev., Father Cosmos Omboto, and other men of God, each one of them shot to death at close range. Weisco had just arrived in the Southern Cameroons with his wife and eight little kids to start God's work. His life is now part of our consciousness, the Southern Cameroons' story, and history.

I was forced to get on board when I realized that I did not know where I came from and where I was going, as a person and as a Southern Cameroonian. My history, had for too long, been completely hidden from me. I studied history as a subject up to high school without knowing the pathetic story of the Southern Cameroons. And that happened to all other generations before me. All we ever learned was about European and world war histories, the history of the French Revolution, the American revolution, Prussian Empire, Russian Empire, the Tsars, Alexander the Great, British Monarchy and their wars, the Holocaust, and so on. We never learned about the Trans-Atlantic slave trade or the history of the Cameroons or that of Cameroun. Yes, there is one spelt with two 'o's and one spelled with a 'un' at the end. A small difference with big consequence for my people. While we were forced-fed the history of everyone else that did not look like us, events next door in Nigeria, Chad, and Ghana, along with other African nations like Ethiopia, Kenya, and South Africa, were not a part of our curriculum.

The ongoing genocide in Ambazonia forced me to find out about my true history. What I discovered shocked me. It was then that I learned that countries like Chad, Gabon, the Republic of Congo, Equatorial Guinea, the Central African Republic, and even parts of Ghana once belonged to one huge German colony, "Kamerun," just like Ambazonia and La Republic du Cameroun. This giant colony was later broken up after World War II and shared between the UK and France.

Ambazonians keep discovering many more hidden truths about their history. As they do, a strong wave is sweeping them off the sea of colonial and neo-colonial oppression, especially from LRC. This hidden history and the question it raises will cause the 'titanic' ship of their slave master to sink. How much more time to wait before the African Union, United Nations, Commonwealth, the International Criminal Court, and other institutions take action to bring justice to the oppressed people of Ambazonia? Of late, some countries have raised their voices, while others pretend not to see. The dangerous tentacles of the disaster in the Southern Cameroons could spread beyond regional frontiers if they continue to delay long-awaited moves for a just unfolding solution to this nightmare.

Below are more reasons why I am fighting for justice and adding a fierce voice to the Southern Cameroons liberation struggle.

Little Ellen Shot at Close Range

One of the worst atrocities that tore my heart into shreds was the brutalized face of a little girl, Ellen. I lost control posting the image of this baby on Facebook, tearfully asking why such monstrosity. Ellen's face was completely shattered. She now has half a face. How God made it possible for her to stand up and let that picture be taken is baffling. It wasn't the kind of wound that she could easily survive. Watching this and many other horrific cases, power wielders, who ought to do something, keep whispering to LRC to take cosmetic actions or remain silent. But their silence only increases the resolve, determination, and persistence of Ambazonians, heavily backed by the restoration forces defending Ground Zero.

Stolen Statehood

This upcoming nation on the West Coast of Africa, will never be the same again. On April 21, 1961, the UN General Assembly session voted overwhelmingly with 64 votes against 23 and 10 abstentions, for the independence of the former British Southern Cameroons. The plebiscite asking us to obtain independence by "joining" Nigeria or La Republique du Cameroun was a poisoned pill. We 'joined' LRC in an illegal federation in 1961. Since then, we have neither been federated nor freed again. This unholy marriage has even lasted far more than we expected. It was never consummated from the very onset, which is why loud echoes for divorce did not delay to start haunting both partners. Until this day, over 90% of the terms of the federation contract have never been respected by LRC. This was supposed to be founded on equality for both parties in the economic, political, cultural, and social space of the common country that the two formed called the Federal Republic of Cameroon.

From the start of the 'joining' to achieving independence for Ambazonia, LRC sought to tactfully assimilate us. First, in 1972, the name "Federal Republic of Cameroon" (created in 1961) was unilaterally changed by the previous LRC President—Ahmadou Ahidjo. A new name (or was it a new country?) emerged—"The United Republic of Cameroon." NO sooner had we, in the Southern Cameroons become accustomed to the new name in 1984, than the next President changed the country's name to "La Republic du Cameroun," essentially leaving the Federation. Paul Biya who has been in power for 37 years, is said to be the one who seceded and unwittingly ended up restoring the independence of the Southern Cameroons as an independent state. Observers say there is no doubt that France is behind all these changes in Africa and in Cameroun.

France is a predatory nation; its claws always in the affairs of

African countries, particularly in French African countries. Had the marriage not been founded on such crooked terms, we would not be in this catastrophe. Our people were fooled to join them through that ugly referendum question whose answer was YES or OUI (French), both meaning the same thing. A confusing proposition imposed on them, one that they never understood. Many left the polling station without knowing what they voted for because of the two tricky responses. The first Prime Minister from SC, Dr. John Ngu Foncha, primary architect of the Southern Cameroon-LRC marriage resigned in frustration in June 1990 over the poor treatment of his people. Like Foncha, S.T. Muna was also accused of betraying the Southern Cameroons into second colonization at the hands of LRC and France. History has it that John Ngu Foncha fought for unification with LRC while the renowned leader, Dr. Endeley strongly objected, opting instead for joining the Federation of Nigeria.

Some historians believe Ahidjo connived with Foncha for a cheap push over. No sooner was the Plebiscite done with, than it was mission accomplished for LRC. LRC set about to dismantle or destroy all the thriving companies and institutions in the Southern Cameroons, replace any influential governing structures, and replace members of its government in strategic positions with French-speaking people. In short, most of our prominent leaders were muscled out of existence as soon as the federation was formed. The Southern Cameroons' economic powerhouses like the Cocoa-Coffee Marketing Board, Cameroon Bank, MIDENO, WADA, Tiko Airport, Bali and Bafut Airports, PowerCam—the Electricity generating company, Tiko Port, Victoria Seaport, Public Works Department, and technological institutions like GTC Ombe and CCAST Bambili were undermined. These were all thriving organizations and institutions that provided services and employment for Southern Cameroonians.

Our fight had begun long before the 2016 lawyers' and teachers' strike. We actually wept, shouted loud, even though jailed or killed for doing so; our blood pressure rose when we saw all these illegal happenings. But no one ever cared to listen. Our people suffered physical torture on top of all that. Many who couldn't stand it abandoned the country, some with whole families, escaped to strange lands where they have been living for several decades. And here is where the colonial masterminds behind all these got us all cheap. Such a big game plan to force us to abandon our country with anger, go to theirs and give all our talents and intellectual know-how to them. At the same time, they are exploiting and draining our resources, just like they drain our brain and talents. When you think it over, you wouldn't want to boast of anything you acquire overseas until you finally get back to your homeland.

The total rape of Ambazonia until its last treasure is taken away seems to be the agenda of its new colonizers—French Cameroun, and their foreign master—France. When the educational and legal systems started being heavily adulterated with French-style education and judges, Ambazonians couldn't take it anymore. In October 2016, teachers and lawyers broke loose. And that is what has catapulted the revolution until this day spearheaded that year by Felix Balla Nkongho who suffered in jail, then Sisiku Ayuk Tabe in 2017, abducted with his entire cabinet by LRC in Abuja. It is now guided finally by Dr Samuel Ikome Sako. Mounting momentum and more reasons to fight with great expectations of victory sparked off with the arrival of the current president of the Interim Government of the Southern Cameroons, Dr Sako. He came with a determined force that has left the enemy dumfounded. In his unmatched focus and resilience to drive his country to total independence, so much has been achieved in mobilizing the people and setting up structures in preparing for the new nation.

The pain of the people of the Southern Cameroons has been excessive. There is no time for whining, not even soon after the war. The various leaders of the revolution must watch every move and decision they make so that they do not intensify the torture and get Ambazonians hobbled for another half-century or a lifetime. Those leaders, multitudes of surrogates and activists who blindly support personalities or partners instead of the cause, without penetrating their dark inner circles to know exactly what evil plans might lurk within, need to watch out.

CHAPTER 8

FROM "CAMEROONIAN" TO PROUD AMBAZONIAN

MARIANTA NDOH

Like many others from the "Northwest and Southwest provinces" of Cameroon, I watched and listened with increasing dismay as events in our homeland unfolded in the watershed year—2016. I had always been very proud and happy to tell anyone that I was from Cameroon. All that has since changed! It has been a slow but heart-breaking journey of discovery. This is my journey of how, when, and why I got involved in the struggle.

Throughout my life, there has always been one form of grievance or another from our people. There had been several initial indications from the people that the government of La Republique du Cameroun (LRC) should start listening more to them. But each time, nothing concrete was done. Lately, I began hearing grumbling from friends and from home that something was wrong. Before many of us could really cue in, the Coffin Revolution, led by Mancho Bibxy, was launched to highlight the plight of our people, and its effects spilled into our homes through TV and social media, and into spaces in the diaspora. Many of us started paying attention to what was happening in the Southern Cameroons. We were happy to hear those teachers and lawyers were standing against the government. They were confronting decades of marginalization, the francophone

67

influence on our education system, and the use of civil law instead of the common law in our courts and legal system. These protests were signs of hope that finally something positive was going to happen. However, to my utter disbelief, our distinguished lawyers and teachers, who courageously stood up for the people, were publicly beaten and humiliated. It was ridiculous that LRC would choose to ignore serious concerns peacefully raised by its 'own people,' albeit from a section of the country. Paul Biya's government chose its favored approach—violent crackdown!

The turning point for me was when we heard about the death of the University of Buea student who had been brutally attacked and raped. This was a parent's worst nightmare! A mother never imagines that, after all the hard work of raising a precious child, she will lose her in such an evil and despicable way. How can one reconcile these atrocities? What did that innocent girl do to deserve such a thing? My questions were just too many to comprehend. My shock turned to dismay and then to outrage. How could the perpetrators of such an act not be brought to justice? How was it that they freely roamed about terrorizing the people whom they call Anglophones and "brothers?"

As actions speak louder than words, LRC's blatant brutality told us that we are not considered citizens of Cameroon. Then, it gradually sunk in. We are not Cameroonians. We are Southern Cameroonians. That was it! That day, I think, like most Southern Cameroonian mothers around the world, I said enough was enough! My mother hen instincts kicked in and there was no turning back. Our children must be protected. Period! I knew I had to be the voice of the voiceless. The pain was unbearable. The tears did not take away the pain. Only one thing could ease the pain—Action! That decision brought about some immediate relief because, for a long time, I had simply worried. For a long time, I and tens of thousands of Southern Cameroonians across the globe, were in a state of collective helplessness. It is one of the most negative emotions a human being should experience. So, making the decision to act, to do something to stem this tidal wave of helplessness, propelled me to embrace empowerment. That decision took some of the weight off my heavy sad heart and shoulders. That decision relieved me to use my brain to engage in thoughtful reflections and actions for the benefit of my people.

With my newfound strength, born out of the determination to stay active, now came many desperate questions requiring answers. With my husband's support, we emailed our first letter to our Member of Parliament (MP) drawing his attention to the gross human rights abuses taking place in Cameroon. We petitioned the MP so that Cameroon should be suspended from the Commonwealth.

Then, we made arrangements for a face-to-face meeting with our MP to find out what he and the UK government were going to do about the war in the Southern Cameroons. One thing was made very clear—the need for coordinated diplomatic efforts to raise awareness about the increasing human-rights violations carried out by LRC against the peaceful citizens of Ambazonia. Community mobilization was geared towards engaging our various MPs. Our desire was for the UK government to discuss this crisis in the British Houses of Parliament. We were advised to set up an All-Party Parliamentary Group (APPG) for Cameroon, comprising of Members of Parliament from all the political parties in the United Kingdom. However, our Member of Parliament could not chair the group, as he had his hands full with other projects. He assured us that he would be happy to be part of the APPG if we could get a chairperson for it. It was encouraging to hear. So, reaching out to other MPs was our next move.

Writing to Members of Parliament was just the start, as more action needed to be taken. A group of us in my city got together and formed the Southern Cameroons Midlands Action Group (SCMAG). Similar groups sprung up in response to the increasing humanitarian crisis in the Southern Cameroons.

The options concerning charting a way forward included maintaining the status quo, federation, independence, or being undecided? Debates were taking place and decisions were being made. You could see that some within the communities made up their minds more easily while others remained either in denial or stood on the fence. This scenario would play out often.

I have a multi-faceted involvement in the revolution. As a mother, wife, and educator, I happily embraced anything within my ability to move the revolution forward, starting from involvement in my local group, soliciting my MPs, setting up a charity, and serving the European and worldwide Country Coordinators leadership and Directorate in the Ambazonian Department of Education. There was little or no coverage in the UK mainstream media on the atrocities going on in Ambazonia by LRC armed forces. Many non-Ambazonians I encountered had no knowledge of our people's plight. From that realization, we founded the *Charity Friends of British Southern Cameroons* whose main purposes were to raise awareness and to mobilize people and opinions outside of Ambazonian communities. In early November 2017, the charity had its first fundraising event. We invited friends, neighbors, and colleagues to our home for afternoon tea with some popular Southern Cameroonian foods like puff-puff, dodo, jollof rice, and chicken. My neighbors and charity trustees were just fabulous. They also cooked and brought along food from other cultures and helped raise the charity's first funds which were then used to purchase charity wristbands. That is how *Friends of British Southern Cameroons* was born. The group continues to raise funds to support the Electronic Food Bank, our refugees, and Internally Displaced People (IDPs) through the Ambazonia Department of Health and Human Services.

I remember when the Interim Government (IG) was formed and later our beloved President Sisiku Ayuk Tabe came to Leicester during his first meet-the-people tour. It was very motivating to see the evolution of our revolution. The people were excited. We now had a government be it interim, a president, and the conceptualization of 'getting to Buea,' the capital of Ambazonia. He spoke the iconic words, 'No one is bigger than this revolution, not even me.' On his second visit to the UK, he called the group leaders together for a meeting and task an electoral committee to organize elections for a UK Leadership team to work with the Interim Government. He advised us to unite behind elected leaders as a solution to the apparent fragmentation in the UK diaspora. Thereafter, I did not really think about the elections again, until the electoral committee put out the information for elections. A little voice within me said, "Run for office," and I asked God how that was going to work? I work full time as a science teacher, and I have to be a mum to four children. Where was I going to find the time to do this? I tried to ignore the voice, but it did not go away. After several days of meditation and fasting, I got an affirmative response from the last two hymns during Mass. The last one touched me the most, so I'll share it with you below. This is one of the most profound religious experiences I have had. It was beautiful and serene. I had tears of joy from the depth and clarity of my response. I could not move for some time. I surrendered everything to Yahweh, the Lord Almighty. I also consulted my husband, my family, and friends. With their blessings, I submitted my candidacy for the UK leadership position in the elections.

One of the hymns reads as follows:

Jesus Christ is waiting,

Waiting in the streets;

No one is his neighbor,

All alone he eats.

Listen, Lord Jesus,

I am lonely too.

Make me, friend or stranger,

Fit to wait on you

Jesus Christ is raging,

Raging in the streets,

Where injustice spirals

And real hope retreats.

Listen, Lord Jesus,

I am angry too.

In the Kingdom's causes

Let me rage with you.

Jesus Christ is healing,

Healing in the streets;

Curing those who suffer,

Touching those he greets.

Listen, Lord Jesus,

I have pity too.

Let my care be active,

Healing just like you.

Jesus Christ is dancing,

Dancing in the streets,

Where each sign of hatred

He, with love, defeats.

Listen, Lord Jesus,

I should triumph too.

On suspicion's graveyard

Let me dance with you.

I have been serving in the Ambazonia leadership within the Directorate in the Education Department, UK Vice Country Coordinator, Chair of European Country Coordinators, and Interim

Chair of the reconstituted Country and Regional Coordinators. I am assisting with the setting up of the Ndian County and its local government area (LGA) structures as well as the Nguti LGA, all of which are coming on very strongly thanks to the dedication and commitment of the people in our revolution. I have been working with the Southern Cameroons Women, UK as a Spokesperson. I know I need to do more on that after our Berlin conference, as the ASSC and County/LGA formation have been my focus for the last few months. In my various roles, I continue to have opportunities to work with a diverse range of Southern Cameroonians. It has been a truly enlightening experience. I am grateful for the leadership training provided to Country Coordinators last year because it has proven to be useful.

As a whole, I can state that the majority of Southern Cameroonians are just wonderful, and I really admire them for the way they work tirelessly, sacrificing their time and financial resources. From Country Coordinators to County/LGAs to Amba Women and constituents, I thank you all from the bottom of my heart for everything you do. Only our good God, who sees everything, will continue to bless you.

It is also certain that our detractors are few, but very loud in their quest to destroy our revolution. Thus, we must remember to put our people first by being patriotic and professional in everything we do. It is our collective duty to defend the lives and dignity of our people. This battle also needs to be fought spiritually. We all know about post-traumatic stress disorder and what we see and hear happening to people every day in Ambazonia is soul-destroying. So, we must put all Ambazonians in our prayers. I would like us to reflect on these two verses of the Bible:

"Pardon the iniquity of this people, I pray thee, according to the greatness of thy steadfast love, and according to thou hast forgiven this people, from Egypt even until now." - Numbers 14:19

'Yet even now,' says the LORD, 'return to me with all your heart, with fasting, with weeping, and with mourning.' - Joel 2:12. There is a real need for Ambazonians to show unity of purpose. There is hope for Ambazonia. I am optimistic that with love, mutual respect, and selflessness we will get to Buea sooner rather than later.

CHAPTER 9

MY PAIN, MY AMBALAND

MA MARY MUMA

Half a century of pounding

our flesh, pain, and agony

Mercilessly inflicted on a people, Ambazonians

Forced to smell the stench of evil all around

Threatened since 1961;

Gifted away to French Cameroun

by colonial masters

Ahidjo was glad to oblige;

glad to be the housekeeper for the French

as the English hurried to their tea rooms in London.

We were thrown into a nightmare;

five decades and counting

Our land, our homes,

our sacred places have been daily desecrated

because we dared to unburden ourselves

from the weights and shackles of enslavement.

We woke up to the sound of gunfire,

a war was unleashed on us

There was chaos and pandemonium everywhere

But every turn we took,

we met with blood thirsty soldiers;

it rained bullets.

We ran in different directions

We ran into each other, into trees,

into treacherous rivers and valleys

and into the mouths of wild animals.

Death was everywhere

The villages fell silent

A mother returns

to see the ruins of her home

Her sister was burnt alive;

her baby thrown into boiling oil

She tries to shout, but she had lost her voice

She sits down on a stone in the courtyard

and stares into the emptiness before her

She drops, broken hearted, unbearable despair

We must fight back

The evil giant in the land must be caged;

so that peace can return

The land must be cleansed

because the blood of our children,

husbands, wives, brothers, sisters and grandparents

has been spilt in this manic and evil madness.

Only then will the heart of Ambazonia beat again; when freedom is won and the stench is gone.

CHAPTER 10

MY AMBA STORY

GERTRUDE KISOB

Hello, my name is Gertrude Kisob, the Chair for the Santa Local Government Area (SLGA). It was tough for me to accept the idea that I would take a position and work within one area in the Ambazonian struggle. I have always been a person with lots of ideas and I often resist being tied down to one position. So, when three members of my team asked me to run for the position, I reluctantly acquiesced to their request. It occurred to me that this might be my opportunity to use my talents and people skills to serve our people. My biggest dream was to see my home, the Southern Cameroons, back on its feet as a vibrant and growing nation instead of being an economic and social wasteland.

My dream was to see the home that I knew growing up; however, the Cameroon I thought I knew is different from what I see today. There were water taps on the roadside with clean water for all. Growing up back home, I remember how the roads, though many not fully tarred, were well maintained. Our food supplies, health facilities, and environment were good. How about the medical facilities? Both public and private hospitals were cleaned and sanitized daily. The medical staffs were professional in every respect. There was discipline and duty consciousness in service. If you were admitted into the hospital, medications were administered by healthcare staff as prescribed. You paid for the medications and services upon discharge. Nowadays, when medications are prescribed, families run out of the hospital to buy them. However, the doctor, without notice, may change the prescription the next day. Patients with little means to pay for health services must either pay facilities in cash first or die needlessly. Back in the day, all our public service sector departments functioned properly. The Public Works Department (PWD) maintained our roads. As far as heath and sanitation was concerned, there were health and sanitation inspectors who ensured that every home had a toilet and that the food sold in the market was of good quality—clean and good enough for human consumption. The meat we consumed was inspected and care was taken to prevent any epidemics. Citizens came to expect these services from their government, and they were dutifully provided to them.

In the countryside, men and women cultivated the fertile soil and planted subsistence crops and cash crops such as coffee and cocoa. These were great sources of income for rural families who earned enough money from their honest labor to afford private boarding secondary schools for their children in towns and cities. Local farmers' cooperatives were set up and trading in cash crops was fair and prices were competitive.

Today, much of our roads in the Southern Cameroons are in poor condition. Our environment is destroyed because of poor urbanization. Our hospitals have become places where people go to die; good and honest doctors lack the barest of equipment and medications to care for the sick. The large tea and coffee plantations have become neglected areas or have been sold to Francophones at give-away prices. The vibrant ones are those in the hands of the ruling party elite, multi- millionaires. Today, women are left to carry the bulk of the burden of fending for their families. The men leave for the cities in search of better paying jobs and there are none to be found for our boys—not in our own land and certainly not in French Cameroon. What a burdensome life!

What if we can recreate the days of old and much more? What if we combine the experiences of the old and add the knowledge of today? I think we can make a better homeland for our children without La Republic du Cameroun (LRC) dragging us backwards and siphoning away everything of value that we have. It has become evident that no matter how long we have lived with LRC, they would always view us as a lower class of people.

Being part of the conversation on the issues facing Ambazonians is nothing new to me. In 1990, when the Social Democratic Front (SDF) party was born, I was in Yaoundé living with my family when some of the founders of the party visited. I recall watching and hoping as students at the University of Yaoundé went on strike to press for social change. I also yearned for change, so much so that I spent six months trying to secure a job at the Social Insurance Fund. And when my name was on the list of applicants selected by the Government of Cameroon to apply to teach at Buea University, I was ecstatic, thinking this was my ticket to return home. Unfortunately, it did not happen.

When Anglophone lawyers and teachers began their protest in 2016, I watched with guarded interest. I later called a friend in Cameroon, who is a teacher, to find out what teachers were doing to stay informed. She put me in touch with Tassang Wilfred, one of the leaders of the Consortium. From that point, I was pleased because I could talk with someone who could give me reliable information about what was happening in the Southern Cameroons.

Now in the United States, I joined a group called *The Strategic Think Tank*. We discussed issues, made plans, and wrote position papers for the struggle. In 2017, a group called 'MoRISC,' formally known as the "Movement for the Restoration of the Independence of Southern Cameroons," had a conference in Washington, DC which I attended. I was one of the speakers at that conference. MoRISC had prepared its resolutions and wanted us to sign onto what they had presented. We refused to endorse their resolutions. I told them that we were all hungry for change and had come from every corner of this great country. If we did not participate in developing any meaningful plans, it would be no use for us to come again in February as they had suggested.

During this trip to Washington, DC, we stopped at Dr. Ebenezer Akwanga's house. He is the valiant leader of the African People's Liberation Movement (APLM) and the Southern Cameroons Defense Forces (SOCADEF). His wife was a gracious hostess and had cooked all kinds of food and entertained us. It was the first time I had eaten fried cassava. Oh, it was nice. We ate it with roast fish. Dr. Akwanga did something special which warmed my heart. He played a taped conversation he had with one of our people in jail. They were discussing the needs of those locked up, and how he had sent money to assist them with feeding. Dr. Akwanga and I had had a heated argument earlier when I criticized some of the things he had written. But on this day in his house, he stood out as the man who had done so much for the revolution. I had a lot of admiration for him.

After the MoRISC craziness in DC, I turned to Tassang Wilfred, who was the head of SCACUF at that time. I proposed that we should have a SCACUF chapter in every state of the United States of America. That way, everyone would recognize SCACUF as a movement for all Ambazonians.

He was pleased and asked me to work on it. I turned to my friends and group members including Dr. Stephen Shemlon and Timothy Mbeseha and shared the idea with them. Dr. Shemlon assisted in grouping the states he knew had the fewest Cameroonian people together. I started calling around to find people who could head groups in their respective states. Before I could go any further, it was time for the Third Conclave. I quickly sent out what I had done so far to both Wilfred Tassang and Milan Atam. After the conclave, I was asked to join a group in Massachusetts that was set up to work on writing a plan for grouping by regions not states as I had done. At the meeting, I was paired with one other person who had done a similar project. Together, we developed the plan called *Ambazonia Ground Operation* which is how the Ambazonia Regions came into being.

Milan Atam later asked me to join the HSS where I recommended that we should have a Facebook Page to share what we were doing and to also seek suggestions about what was needed. I started requesting assistance from non-Ambazonians and received some money. Lastly, I developed a plan to assist in Nigeria to organize our people into groups of fifty. That way supplies brought into a camp would be given to the leaders in that camp to distribute to their fifty refugee family groups. I thought it would be a good way to prevent our people from queuing up to wait for food. It would also assist in information gathering, especially if we wanted to know how many pregnant women, sick people, and newborn babies were in the camp as well as any other information that we considered necessary. I thought that if one person was responsible for fifty people, they would easily have and provide such information.

Before President Sisiku Ayuk Tabe visited the USA, I was

included in the planning committee where I recommended that instead of us all visiting our leaders in DC, they should visit us in our states of residence. That way more people would see them, and more donations could be collected instead of sending a few people to DC and spending so much on hotels, food, and transportation. That recommendation was taken, and after our leaders visited us locally, we all felt like we were part of the movement.

During the President's last visit to Atlanta, where I was present, I discussed my recommendations with him. I recommended the blocking of roads in Ambazonia with logs, rocks, or anything to prevent the military from reaching our people in our homeland. I also recommended degrading the fighting force of LRC in any way possible before they could reach our towns and villages. "Destroy or attack them before they can get to their intended destination," was my motto. My second battle plan was to prevent the exportation of any of our resources including rubber, timber, oil, cocoa, and coffee from our country.

When Dr. Sako was elected to be captain of the Ambazonian ship, I was elated. Yes, it was because I used to listen to his show: "Dr. Common Sense" and we had similar views on issues of the day. The first opportunity I had to catch him on the phone, I asked him if he was going to implement the plan he talked about on his show; the plan to prevent the exportation of raw materials and all our resources. He assured me that he would implement everything he talked about on his show.

My plea to the international community is to help Southern Cameroonians because we are an innovative people with a great potential to impact this world. Living in a country where our skills are undermined or diminished, where our resources are used for others; living in a country where we are treated as if we do not

84

belong, is debilitating to one's soul and self-esteem. Assisting in our liberation struggle will help us share our God-given talents with the rest of the world. Our children will stand and walk tall and be part of a community where they truly belong.

My message to future generations of Ambazonians is to enjoy their land. We are fighting for them to have freedom and they should never take that for granted. Every time they do something, they should consider whether it benefits their country and if it is worthy of our current fight. I want our future generations to enjoy but judiciously guard what we fought for, always thinking of generations to come.

God Bless Ambazonians!

CHAPTER 11

STANDING TALL FOR AMBAZONIA

COMFORT KONFOR

The quest for Ambazonia independence started in 1953 when our forefathers staged a walkout from the House of Assembly in Enugu, after they were scorned in that parliament by their Nigerian counterparts. In 2016, when lawyers and teachers brought activities in the city of Bamenda to a standstill, because of their disenchantment over the use of the French language in the Southern Cameroons courts and schools, it seemed to me that there was nothing to write home about. I was indifferent because I thought that it was a normal thing to protest, an exercise in freedom of expression, perhaps, a civic duty. But something finally got me off my seat, and that was when I stood up and started asking myself, "Where am I?" "What is happening?" "Why?" It was not a dream. It was real. It was painfully true—girls were being raped, and university students were being dragged in sewage water by the brutal trigger-happy forces of La Republique du Cameroun's (LRC) Rapid Intervention Brigade—BIR as abbreviated in French.

Each time an Ambazonian woman is raped, I see three women being raped and I grieve three times. The day the seventeen-year-old mother was raped in Bamenda by a ruthless soldier, it brought this crime into sharper focus. I wept with her. I am sure other people did. How could I have continued to fold my arms and watch history unfold in the wrong direction? How could I have kept quiet when soldiers violate the dignity of my sisters or deprive them of voices to cry out to the world? How could I have said it did not matter? I will fight until victory is achieved.

The third quarter of 2017 was a phase in our revolution that no Ambazonian will ever forget. In preparation for a worldwide protest on September 22nd of that year, the Takumbeng was unleashed under the leadership of Sisiku Julius Ayuk Tabe. Our revolution caught the world's attention when Ambazonian women, both at home and abroad, led a protest when the United Nations General Assembly (UNGA) was holding. This was a day that Ambazonian women came out in large numbers, dressed in red and white, and led a world protest to tell the United Nations that: 'enough is enough.' This was the day our people, especially those at home, showed the world that they were a peace-loving people, by marching with peace plants and chanting, *"No Violence"* in every town and village in Ambazonia. However, this was the day, King Paul Biya of LRC heartlessly ordered his depraved soldiers to kill our people just to sustain his dictatorship. Unfortunately for him, our people did not give up. That was why they came out again en masse on the 1st of October 2017 to declare the restoration of their stolen independence.

Paul Biya did not hesitate. He did the thing he does best—shooting and killing innocent people. By then, this son of a catechist, Bi Mvondo, was still underestimating our determination. The struggle went on till the 30th of November 2017 when he declared war on Southern Cameroonians. In spite of the thousands of Ambazonian lives lost and thousands arbitrarily arrested, despite the countless mass graves and the scorched-earth policy which has reduced some of our people to 'early man' status as they now reside in bushes, the resilience of our people has not dwindled one bit. Let me stop here and applaud the work of the Department of Health and Social Services (HSS) under the leadership of Secretary of State, Caleche Bongo. The department has done a marvelous job of reaching out to our people, the refugees in Nigeria and the Internally Displaced Persons (IDPs) back in Ambazonia. Another group of women who did a formidable job are the Takembeng Relief Service (TRS), under the leadership of Professor Elizabeth Ambe. They raised funds, buried our dead, provided medical assistance to the wounded in hospitals, and also showed love to the immediate families of our fallen heroes. History shall never forget you ladies.

Since 2016, a series of shocking things have happened. So many that I have lost count. The arrest of Sisiku Julius Ayuk Tabe and his associates was a heavy burden for me to bear. Let me stop here to say a bit about my interactions with some of our abducted leaders. The last time I spoke with Sisiku was on the second of January 2018 when I sent him the audio of the pidgin version of his 2017 end-of-year speech, which I had interpreted. He said to me, "Comfort, you are an angel. I cannot thank you enough." Each time I replay the tape and hear his voice, what I tell myself is that: "All is not lost." I am standing tall for him. As for Pa Nfor Ngala Nfor, I can call him my father. We have known each other for a very long time. He has mentored me throughout my life. The last time we spoke was when he called me after listening to a series of audios and watched videos which I had done in my language to educate my people about our revolution. He is such a sweet daddy. I can never forget this day. He started by making me understand how proud he was of me, for undertaking such initiative to educate our people in our native language. However, he said that there were some mistakes he wanted to point out. But the mistakes made both of us laugh. I'm smiling as I write. Pa had been making notes as he listened to my messages, so he could read out some of the phrases. He then said, "This was pure

English, Comfort". There was no iota of "Limbum" in that phrase," he 'complained.' He then taught me how to refer to the French language in Limbum, which literally translated to "language of the frogs." The most interesting thing was when he taught me how to say 1961 in our language. I am giggling. I wish I could boast that I can say it. I wish I knew that these bullies were going to take him away from me when they were abducted in Nigeria.

The abduction came like a thief, no one expected it to happen. But I have not lost any ounce of my determination. This got me more radicalized instead. Each time I feel like giving up, I am aware that another woman is being raped. How can I give up when this independence fight is not yet over? How can I even stop fighting when Sisiku and his aides are still in detention? Who will fight for them? Who will tell the world about the impunity and atrocities in the Southern Cameroons? Who will remind the world about the burning alive of our elder, Mami Api?

In the beginning, I thought that the brutal crackdown would stop. But the reality is that Paul Biya's thugs are on a mission - to see that Ambazonia is wiped out. I became even more frustrated with the burning of over 200 villages in our homeland. The summary execution of young Ambazonian men and women from Menka-Pinyin to Bali Nyonga, to Widikum, to Mayo Binka, made me feel even more frustrated. Despite these atrocities, I have never felt the urge to throw in the towel. I fight on, till' the last Ambazonian is set free. I will fight for Sam Soya. I will fight for Mancho Bibixy. I will fight for Patrick Ndangoh. I will fight for General Ivo. I will fight for General Bea-Bea. I will fight for all the fallen heroes of the Ambazonia Restoration.   I am weeping as I call out their names. You fought a good fight my heroes. Rest ye well.

Ambazonia shall live to remember you. I am standing tall for

Ambazonia because you have laid a solid and unbreakable foundation on which an unshakable Ambazonia shall be erected—an Ambazonia that shall be the shining star of Africa. Thank you, my heroes.

Despite the deplorable ordeals we have experienced, there are some things that give me reason to continue fighting. One of my greatest sources of inspiration was, and is, Barrister Nalova, (going forward, I will call her Nalo). She is a woman I really respect. Nalo is that lady whom I would like to refer to as a rare gem of womanhood. She is so courageous that my words cannot adequately explain. Nalo is not only a lawyer but also a single mum. Nalo is that single mum who abandoned her two-year-old toddler, her less-than-a-year-old baby, and her babysitter to the mercy of anyone who cared, in order to escape for her dear life, because she stood tall to defend the motherland.

Nalo did not care about the wellbeing of her children, but she cared about the wellbeing of eight million Ambazonians. Apparently, she must have thought that "my children and babysitter are only three out of the eight million." If not so, she should have stopped the fight and stayed to protect her career and family. With all her accounts frozen, Nalo was left with 300 CFA francs in her purse. Was she going to use this money to buy food for her children, or for her own upkeep? She had to leave when it was apparently whispered into her ear that she was being sought for arrest by Biya's murderous thugs. Nalo was smuggled by a 'good Samaritan,' in the boot of his car like luggage, into the middle of nowhere, and she finally found herself in Nigeria. What happened to her children and the babysitter? No one wanted to be seen anywhere around them, for fear of being prosecuted. But what baffles me was the fact that Nalo did not give up. She kept fighting. That was why she was the only woman among the Nera 12 who was abducted in Nigeria. But why recount Nalo's story when everybody knows about it? It is just a reminder. Reminding fellow Ambazonians and the world that in spite of what she went through, the only reward she got was castigation. But what I admire is the fact that Nalo still stands tall for Ambazonia. That is why I am still standing tall by her side.

I am standing tall for Ambazonia because Eileen Wifengla made me to do just that. I have never, and may never, understand why Eileen kept smiling, despite her pain and her disfigured face. I keep asking myself the question—if Eileen can smile, what reason do I have not to smile? I believe that if Eileen did not have Ambazonia at heart, she would have given up on life. She would surely have died. But she lived, not just living, but permanently wearing a smile, making me surmise that she smiles because Ambazonia is real, and that there is hope. Eileen Wifengla to me is the ray of Ambazonian hope for a brighter future. Kaddy Cisse made me stand tall. She is one of the ladies who give me reasons to fight on. She is not of Ambazonian descent. She took it upon herself to courageously fight to free Ambazonia. She is that woman that will look at the dictator at Etoudi, Paul Biya, straight in his eyes, anytime, anywhere and call his crime by its name. She took the risk. She risked the lives of her family members back home, just to see Ambazonia free. What stops me then from standing tall? All I can say is thank you Kaddy Cisse.

There was a period in the Ambazonia war of independence that the Southern Cameroonian women in North America stood tall and moved mountains just to see Ambazonia become a reality. I remember the first protest in Washington DC, in front of the White House. Vy Mbanwei spoke and almost lost her voice; Mami Gera, Abu Fri, and the rest of the women were soaked by rain when they were half-dressed just to draw public attention to the fact that they

91

were grieving. These ladies did not, however, go unnoticed for standing up to fight for our people. Their efforts were met with cyber-bullying, yet they did not give up. I am proud of Abu Fri, for the one-woman demonstration she staged in front of the United Nations.

Ambazonian women in Europe were not left out. I should show love and respect to Dr. Bernadette Ateghang, Gillian Esua, Emma Larry, Paulette Mengjo, Eleanor, Dora Gorim, and many others for their dedication. I wish I could call all the names. They have always been present at demonstrations from Germany to Geneva and London. You all have stood the test of time. Only God knows how you have been managing your time running a challenging revolution like ours—being wives and mothers and going to work as well. God bless your efforts. Special tribute to fellow women of Ambazonia! They have chosen to put their lives on hold and to take up crude tools to fight and defend the motherland. For the first time let me call them "Amba Girls."

Mark Bareta and Tapang Ivo Tanu stood tall for Ambazonia when all hope seemed to be lost. Both of them were the interim leaders of the consortium when the consortium members under the leadership of Barrister Agbor Balla, were arrested by the Biya government for demanding their fundamental human rights. They did a phenomenal job! Ambazonians know that. No one could have done it better. Many things have gone wrong since then, but it remains a fact that they served Ambazonians when they needed their services. Thank you, brothers! Eric Tataw also stepped in somewhere along the line and has been consistent in his efforts to see Ambazonia succeed. He is one of the activists who have taken everyone to task—from members of the Interim Government (IG) to leaders of the political movements of the revolution. He is known for his slogan,

"My name is Eric Tataw, quote me anywhere." He has been doing much in educating as well as encouraging fellow Ambazonians that their cause is genuine and that they should not give up. I can quote him anywhere for standing tall for Ambazonia.

Special thanks to some of our social media activists. I wish I could mention all of you by name. Though faceless, Kemi Ashu's hand in the revolution has been very visible and worth mentioning. She did a great job of providing first-class and genuine information from home, putting our people on alert about the presence of the wicked killer forces of La Republique du Cameroun. The resistance and persistence of our activists is proof that Buea is real. Despite their differences, they have been pressing on homewards. You have stood the test of time by standing tall for Ambazonia. Posterity will remember you all. I cannot wait to meet you all face-to-face in Buea and as soon as possible.

When President Sisiku Ayuk Tabe and his cabinet members were abducted, Ambazonians thought it was the end of the revolution. But behold, Acting President Samuel Ikome Sako courageously accepted to bear the crown of thorns. The coming of Acting President Sako was a new dawn. That was the birth of ground action in Ambazonia. This rekindled my spirit and gave me more reason to fight on till victory is won. I pledge my loyalty to our Interim Government, be it under Dr. Sako or when Sisiku comes back. It is not a perfect government, obviously, because it is run by imperfect human beings. All they need as a government in exile is the support of every Ambazonian.

Students are the other set of people who have paid the price for our freedom. The truth about life is that it takes sacrifice to achieve many things. The world does not need a clairvoyant to tell how much you have sacrificed for the Ambazonian revolution: your education, your virginity, your dignity as humans, your family, and friends. One thing I would like you to know is that you are special, you are unique. You are the chosen generation. Count it a blessing that you had this rare opportunity to be actively involved in the quest for Ambazonia's freedom. One thing I will never stop telling you is that you should beware of the evil forces of Biya's military. These bullies carry weapons of mass destruction around their loins, that is, the gun and their manhood. If they do not shoot and kill or maim you, they will rape you, contaminate you with their deadly sexually transmissible diseases or get you pregnant.

It is frustrating that you cannot go to school now, and it is well understood. What matters now is your safety and wellbeing, your lives. Stay away from harm's way, go to church when it is time to go to church, go with mum to the farm, to her hairdresser's, or to the market, and help in whatever thing she is doing. Go with dad to the garage or to the shop, or wherever he is going that is safe. Be keepers of one another. The Ambazonia war of independence has led all Ambazonians to become one family. Each time an Ambazonian man is killed, all Ambazonian ladies mourn a husband, a son, a brother, a father, and a friend in that fallen hero. When Ambazonians in the diaspora send support, they send it to all 'our internally displaced persons and refugees.'

The picture of Ambazonia that I have in mind is a beautiful and lovely one. As a family, we shall make it happen. Thank you, fellow sisters, on ground zero, for sacrificing your husbands! We in the diaspora have your backs. Thank you, children, for sacrificing your parents so that we can have our freedom! God bless you mothers, fathers, brothers, and sisters for sacrificing so that we can be free. Thank you, students, for sacrificing your education so that we can have our independence restored! Thank you to the restoration forces for putting your lives on hold in exchange for the restoration of our independence.

It would be unfair to talk about the Ambazonian quest for the restoration of their sovereignty without mentioning some of our revolutionaries and human rights activists like Boh Herbert, Lucas, and Ebenezer Akwanga. Individually and at some point, as a team, they have been nightmares to the regime at Etoudi. I consider them to be the protagonists of this revolution. In spite of the differences that exist among us, they are still doing a lot. However, much more can be done if we put our differences and interests aside and think and plan from the same platform with our interim Government (IG). What we Ambazonians want now is a free Ambazonia.

In this independence fight, we have all been learning on the job and doing a great job. The existential cry is this: "We should collaborate and get this mess out of our way. Stand tall for Ambazonia." Life is sweeter at home than anywhere else. We are up to the task.

Long live the Federal Republic of Ambazonia. Short live the war.

CHAPTER 12

THE AMBAZONIAN REVOLUTION: A NEVER-ENDING NIGHTMARE

VICTORINE YANGNI

I remember it vividly. It was an evening in 2016. I was reading my WhatsApp messages. I came across a report about lawyers striking in Cameroon. They held placards with slogans and were wearing their lawyers' robes. As I read, I wondered, what is going on here? Then, I watched a video of the police pulling one of the lawyers down the street like a rag doll. Other videos showed lawyers marching in streets in other Southern Cameroonian towns to demand changes to the legal system. It was then that I realized that something serious was happening in the place I called my country; the country I left not long after graduating from high school.

You see, I grew up in the Southern Cameroons, the part of Cameroon now at war. As a citizen of Cameroon, I studied European history more than I studied my own. I vaguely remember the businesses and establishments we had back then because they are since long gone. There was a Produce Marketing Board, Public Works Department (PWD), the Cameroon Bank, and many other thriving businesses in the Southern Cameroons. They died leaving no footprints. There was much more than that. I remember my grandfather's coffee farms and how people used to bring their coffee beans to him to be ground. We had so much land and much of it was used to grow coffee plants. But these are now just memories, memories that events in the Southern Cameroons have resurfaced for me, and I am sure for many others. We used to harvest the coffee beans and soak the ripe ones. They had a sweet taste. Then, for some reason, the coffee plants were left to dry up and were eventually cut down. I wondered why. Yes, I wondered, but for some reason, I just never asked. Maybe it was because back then children weren't allowed to ask too many questions.

But now it's 2016 and back in Cameroon, trouble was brewing. I remember reading many messages about teachers and lawyers going on strikes. I also heard of students protesting, taking to the streets, and being chased off by tear gas.   Hearing about professionals protesting, led me to believe that something serious was about to happen. I had the feeling that change was coming and that I needed to pay close attention to the events unfolding in Cameroon. Then things started getting really tense when the lawyers and teachers, who were now an organized Consortium, went into negotiations with the government of La Republique du Cameroun.

At first, I watched with others as the situation became more and more tense. It was after the Consortium leaders were jailed in 2016 that I joined the struggle. I remember getting a call from a friend. She informed me that the members of our Houston, Texas group were also organizing a strike to demonstrate in front of our City Hall in support of the struggle. I joined them to make my voice heard. I knew I had to be heard too. This was a revolution for change in the Southern Cameroons. And I knew that it was necessary. I attended that first rally in front of the Houston City Hall. From then, I never missed any of the other four rallies we held in front of the French Consulate. Later, I joined the newly formed Houston Support the Struggle of Southern Cameroon (HSSSC), a humanitarian group of concerned Southern Cameroonians in Houston. I quickly became very involved as one of the organizers. We later arranged a huge Town Hall meeting inviting activists to speak on the Southern Cameroons. That event was followed by another town hall meeting during which we gave the Interim President, Ayuk Tabe a welcome fit for a President. It was a huge success, as Southern Cameroonians gathered to hear his vision for the people of the Southern Cameroons. We met to assess the Southern Cameroonian situation and to update the community. We had a fundraiser to collect donations for the refugees in Nigeria. I was responsible for channeling the donations to the appropriate quarters for utilization.

The Direction of the Revolution Changed

Acting Interim President (AIP), Sako Ikome came to town. It was during the AIP's visit that we realized that the direction of the revolution had changed. Its voice too had changed. So too its temperament. It had gone from pleading to international bodies like the United Nations (UN), the African Union (AU), and having one rally after another, to self-defense.

Why I Became Involved: Helping the Vulnerable

When your back is up against the wall and your enemy faces you down, you have no other choice but to fight back or be killed. Ambazonians were backed up against the wall. They chose to fight back with all the strength and dignity from God almighty, who we believe, has ordained our independence struggle. I knew that God did not want His children of Ambazonia to continue in a failed and illegal union with La Republic du Cameroun, a union that for almost six decades brought nothing but pain and suffering to the people. For this reason, I knew the time had come for me to add my voice to the millions of other voices around the world and say, "Yes!" to freedom and "No!" to the torture and the slaughter of our people. It was in this spirit that I boarded a plane to Washington DC to attend a rally in front of the African Union (AU) where our group delivered our grievances and made our request for AU intervention.

My decision to join that first rally in front of the City Hall in Houston was not difficult to make. I figured I was doing what I normally do, which is stand up for the vulnerable people in society. For me, if someone needs help to reach their full potential, I lend them a hand so they can stand on their own feet. When I got involved in this struggle, I was already involved in an organization whose mission it was to help vulnerable women and children. Although part of the organization was spread across Ambazonia, Europe, and the United States, our own branch, here, which is just a small group of women, has managed to build a school in a remote village in the Southern Cameroons. Our organization believes that if we provide education to children and help mothers, it will go a long way in helping families.

Later, we organized our final Town Hall meeting to bring the AIP, Sako Ikome to town. It was during the AIP's visit that we realized that the direction of the revolution had changed. Its voice too had changed. So too its temperament! It had gone from pleading to international bodies like the United Nations (UN), the African Union (AU) and having one rally after another, to self-defense.

My involvement in the Ambazonia fight for freedom is a fight dedicated to giving the people of Ambazonia a voice so that they can express themselves freely. This is because, with a voice, they have choices. With freedom comes the opportunity to seek equal representation. In seeking equal representation, the people of Ambazonia can demand fair treatment and equal rights for their people. Equal rights then give people access to good-paying jobs and to professional schools without bribery. Look at what the people of Ambazonia have been through since entering an ill-fated Federation with French Cameroun.

Independence: Giving People a Voice

Independence provides the children of Ambazonia a voice to decide what kind of education they want. Independence gives our retiring compatriots a chance to go to an office near their homes to access their pensions and not have to travel to a strange city where no one understands their language. It spares our people insults, insults from people who are supposed to help them, but instead mock them as they struggle to speak French. This happens when a language is forced on a people by a country that wants to prevent them from fully participating, in the things that matter to them. Indeed, this essentially bars them from living fully as human beings in their own land

Human Rights Violations

The revolution has been inspirational; there have been many painful moments. Although I had already prepared my mind that the revolution may take a long time, I could never have imagined the silence of the international community towards our plight until recently. It was painful to see how many rallies Southern Cameroonians organized all over the world for nearly three years before some people began to take notice. It appears that we are now finally getting the international community to speak up against all the human rights violations taking place in the Southern Cameroons. Violations on such a scale that if they had happened elsewhere, the perpetrators would have been bombed and held accountable. These violations have included the senseless killing of thousands of our young boys who have decided to stand up to the oppressor in order to save Ambazonia and wrest their freedom from their enemies. They are our valiant fighters, the "Amba boys." We have all seen pictures of lifeless bodies, mostly young men, who only wanted freedom and a land to call their own.

I see houses burned to the ground and old people crying beside them because their lives have been cruelly cut short. The old people left behind don't have the strength to rebuild. When I see this, I just want to keep going!

When I wake up and see another lifeless body and blood flowing all over the Ambazonia soil, I want to keep going! When I see young girls crying so desperately for help after being raped by stone-hearted soldiers, I just want to keep going! When I see young university girls dragged through sewage, I just want to keep going!

When I see a young man with his head being buried in mud, hands and feet tied and Biya's soldiers stepping on his neck while others hit his feet and hold a chair over him so he cannot escape, I want to keep going!

When I see a military truck going through a city spraying bullets at empty buildings, I want to keep going! When I see a human body beaten and chopped into pieces, I want to keep going! When I see women giving birth in the bushes under banana trees, I want to keep going! When I see a helpless child, who does not know where his parents are and is being cared for by a stranger, I want to keep going! When I see a mother crying over her dead child covered in blood, I want to keep going! When I see another lifeless body on the streets of Ambazonia, I cry, then I say to myself, I need to keep going. For if I stop, what will happen? Who will remind the world about what happened to them? Who will celebrate their sacrifices? Who will sing an ode to the fallen Ambazonian?

The International Community is starting to Speak Up

Although it took nearly three years, it was exciting to wake up to the news that a United States Ambassador, Mr. Tibor Nagy, was visiting Cameroon to discuss, among other things, the plight of the Ambazonian people. This news is great because Ambassador Tibor is very knowledgeable about the human rights violations that have been going on in the Southern Cameroons. The Ambassador has also reported that he had received many pictures and videos of the atrocities committed by French Cameroun soldiers. He also acknowledged the concerns of people to the American government about all the human rights violations by Cameroon. I am so proud because finally a superpower is not just speaking out but is prepared to take action.

Another proud moment was when members of the British Parliament openly condemned the regime in Cameroun for its human rights abuses. They had joined their voices with those of other countries to condemn the atrocities being perpetrated in the Southern Cameroons.

Suffering of Youth: The Price of Freedom

The kind of freedom we enjoy in the United States may come to Ambazonians at a very heavy price—the loss of our children, our homes, and our freedom.

For others, it has been torture of the worse kind imaginable. For those who are fighting to free their homeland, all the fallen heroes, all the women who have been raped, all the children born in the bushes, all the children born in refugee camps,I have a message for you: "Your resilience will never be forgotten, your suffering will never be forgotten." To our future generations, you should know that like AIP Sako said: we are the "Do-Something Generation," and we will not leave the liberation of Ambazonia to the future. We will resist now until freedom comes. We shall resist because Ambazonia is our God-given land, and this is a God-ordained revolution, and we MUST succeed.

Why We Want free Amazonia for our Yout

We must succeed because a free Ambazonia awaits us. A free Ambazonia means freedom of speech, press, and assembly. It means access to a decent education for our youth and jobs upon graduation from school, not just for a few privileged individuals. A free Ambazonia means young people will no longer drown in their numbers as they try to cross perilous seas and oceans to go to foreign countries for jobs and some kind of paradise. A free Ambazonia will be a place of opportunities and fair competition. A free Ambazonia will be a place where you can use your creativity and showcase your talent on national and international stages. A free Ambazonia will mean good roads, affordable education, and a chance to stay in school in your own country—yes, a chance to acquire world-class education.

A free Ambazonia will ensure good life expectancy, as health care will be of better quality, and it will be affordable. A free Ambazonia means your talent will be rewarded and your skills utilized to their full extent. The Ambazonia we strive for is one that values freedom. We will build the country we want, with the help of the international community.

CHAPTER 13

PERPLEXITY! THE CRY OF AN AMBAZONIAN MOTHER

MA ELI JAMBELELE

Bewilderment reigns

As blood flows unabating

in that once-upon-a-time oasis of peace

I cannot describe it

Words fail to convey my story!

In a land whose shores pulsate with seafood and vegetation

Abundance to feed thousands of generations,

Lie the hungry, the starving, the tortured of Ambazonia!

And the world looks on – in stony silence

Icy cold and untouched by the ferocity of the looters and killers!

I weep, I moan as I see my children lying there,

piled, one upon the other, like lifeless logs,

In dungeons that

Nature itself has been unwilling to make -

Yet gladly devised for my offspring,

By men they trusted and called compatriots,

Men who fight tooth and nail to wrest away from my descendants their heritage

And these ferocious beasts

They tear to bits

My children's limbs – with the world looking on…

Silent, Cold, Unmoved by our tragedy

While those compatriots

—the name their greedy leader

gave us with his eye on our inheritance –

ferociously wield their guns and knives,

and chop off my infants' heads like croakers.

Hai-yahhhi!

My stomach aches, my feeble limbs falter!

How can I weep? How can I live

with my children slaughtered like pigs?

And my nurslings torn away from my breast

and crushed like chicks by vampires

more wicked than ever seen.

Yet watched, all the while,

by the cold stares of a world

unwilling to stretch the hand

of justice to "the African child"

for whom togetherness defines life

There they lie - my youngsters, my toddlers,

 the dead and the anguished.

Those whose groans strike

the hard wall of human apathy—

My babies – they pass away in despair!

Help! Wipe away the tears of an African mother,

The Ambazonian woman appeals to you,

brothers with consciences touched by the fear of God,

Help! Help sisters all over the world,

You who are mothers,

Dare to be different

and look political injustice

and social greed in the face.

Shy not away from your human duty!

Take off your masks, I plead

And awaken to the plight

of young people cut short in life

for wrestling for their human rights.

For all they want is life and liberty!

CHAPTER 14

IN THE LINE OF DUTY

ANNE NDEH

I have often heard of the Southern Cameroon National Council (SCNC) but knew nothing about this organization. I first got associated with the SCNC when I found myself in Europe under the same roof with a man who had an unending zeal for it. I remember in early 2011 when he offered to take our one-year-old daughter to one of their regional meetings. This was the worst day of my life as his partner. I told him my daughter will not be part of that thing. I despised the SCNC.

A couple of months after that, my partner was busy preparing one morning to go and pick up a very important person who had arrived from ground zero, a man who was coming to attend some high-profile meetings with him. I was curious about whom that man was, but my partner kept shoving me aside. He said the man might be linked to politics. I didn't give a damn about who this man was, but I saw that this man meant everything to my partner. He was so busy making calls and preparing himself to receive the man in question. I tried hard to avoid being part of it all, but he could not stop telling me to be positive because they were fighting to remove a log of wood from the eyes of blind people like me.

One Monday morning before leaving for work, I saw my partner dressed in a suit, so elegant and very eager to go out. I looked at him in a sarcastic way. But he held my left hand, pulled me a little closer to him, and asked me in a very polite way to prepare supper with his visitor in mind. He even added the word "please." To me, he sounded a little frustrated perhaps because he knew I did not want to welcome this man to our home. After seeing the look on his face, I nodded and assured him that I would do what he wanted. My mum always told us when we were growing up that sharing your meal with someone else is a blessing to you than the receiver. I adopted this philosophy, and I have had no regrets for doing so since.

After work, I cooked supper and set the table for three. My partner returned home with one man who looked older than my dad. But my observation was that he looked psychologically stronger than I or my husband. He appeared to be a determined individual. He was soft-spoken. The two men did most of the talking about the events relating to their outing. I admired the charisma of our guest. He caught my attention each time he spoke.

I quickly rushed to the sofa to continue watching the film I had left halfway when they came in from their meeting. The man hummed the song that was playing in the film. "Oh, what a great film," he said. With a lot of surprise, my partner asked him if he knew the film. He said, "Of course. Who hasn't watched the Godfather?" In shock, I turned to look at him. This was because, despite his age and his busy schedule from what I could surmise, he still found time for pleasure. How he coped with all of these, I wondered. He must be an all-around man. For the first time, I turned to him and asked him what he thought about the SCNC and what it could achieve for them. He had been addressing me as "My daughter" since he arrived at our home. He asked me to come sit by him at the table. He took time and lectured me on things that I had never thought about. He asked, "My daughter, which is your country?"

To which I replied, "Cameroon of course."

He looked at me and smiled. This time, he said, "Mum, your generation was denied the true history of your country. The Southern Cameroons is just a victim of neocolonialism. We are a nation doomed to be a victim of modern-day slavery, discrimination, and exploitation without us seeing it," he stated. I opened my mouth to speak, but he quickly fired a series of questions at me: "Have you asked yourself why you had to pass through La Republic du Cameroon before coming to Europe? What happened to your airports?"

I told him Bafut airport is under renovation. I had even forgotten that the Southern Cameroons had international airports. He turned and told my partner to take the time to educate me. I felt so empty but didn't want to admit it.

It was getting late, and he told my partner not to forget that one Sama Thomas was waiting for him. I went into the room and my partner came in and asked me if I could accompany him to Linkerover to drop Pa Nfor Ngalla Nfor so that we could drive back home together. Of course, I was ready to do it because I believed I would still talk with him on the way and find a chance to also make a reasonable point. But he kept feeding me with facts. It was like I had just recovered from Alfred Tennyson's mysterious "Lotos Land" in one of his poems "The Lotos-Eaters."

In late 2016, I was planning to take my third daughter home for the Christmas holidays so that my parents could see her for the first time. I had named her Kristy because that was my mother's name. She was just one year old. Just when I was about to make the flight reservations, I heard about the lawyers' strike that just turned violent in Buea. Common law lawyers had only gone out to demand the withdrawal of French Cameroun magistrates and judges from our courts but were met with violence and arrests. It was a simple request. It was disheartening that in a country with two different languages, two judicial systems, civil law magistrates who only spoke French, were sent to common law courts in the Southern Cameroons where magistrates and legal practitioners could only speak English. To me, it was a grossly provocative situation, a travesty. Just as Southern Cameroonians were trying to understand why their lawyers were beaten, molested, and humiliated, the Southern Cameroons teachers sent out a public notice that they would be joining the lawyers to protest. In a purely Anglo-Saxon system of education, Francophone teachers who could not say "Good Morning" in English were posted to teach students who also could neither speak nor understand French.

The teachers' strike was worse than that of the lawyers. There was pandemonium everywhere. Lawyers declared "no courts," while teachers declared "no schools" until their demands were met. We did not know that pain and sorrow lurked around the corner. It was the breaking point. We saw photos, watched videos, and listened to audios and live broadcasts of university students who went out to protest being beaten, arrested, maimed, and forced to roll in sewage. Some were raped and they died in the process. They were all victims of a brutal mob, soldiers from French Cameroon.

This touched me so much that I reflected on the words of a hero, Pa Nfor Ngalla Nfor, who once told me I was blind. Yes, he had a point. I was still torn between traveling with my one-year-old daughter to a violent environment or staying and waiting for things to calm down. After a second thought, I decided to take the bull by the horns. Yes, I would travel. I was neither a lawyer nor a teacher. How did this concern me? I remembered the strike that took place at Yaoundé University in 2004, which I blindly took part in, only to hear later that the strike leaders collected bribes and vanished. So, I decided that nothing was going to stop me from taking my baby to see my mum as promised.

The next day, I searched and found a very good flight. I called her father to confirm the date and time and asked if it was convenient for him to drop us off and pick us up from the airport upon our return. He told me not to pay for the flight first. He forwarded a video that made me speechless for half-an-hour. I felt as if my blood flow had paused. Then he asked me to decide if I would still take the risk of travelling with an innocent child. The images of boys murdered that day in Bamenda, the sound of guns, the stampede, the bloodshed, the victims, the dead, the wounded left me immobilized, speechless.

I canceled my journey, but I still believed that things would eventually calm down and I would go home with my daughter. In late November 2016, the previous National Chairman for SCNC Belgium convened an emergency meeting. I still do not understand why I was the first lady to call other ladies to hurry up and attend the meeting. I was so involved that I forgot my previous misgivings about SCNC. What a strange world we are living in! Our house was small. Another meeting was scheduled a few weeks later and a host was needed. To my great shock, my family was the next host. I was surprised but didn't object to the idea of playing host to another SCNC meeting.

There was an urgent need for an executive to lead the revolution in Belgium. My partner was appointed chairman, while I was forced to accept a position in the communications department. He was shocked that I didn't object to the nomination. I thought about all the great women who struggled alongside their husbands—Margaret

Thatcher, Theresa May, Winnie Mandela, Hilary Clinton, Ellen Johnson—the list is long. "Yea, I am doing it for those girls and boys who have been murdered in cold blood," I told my husband. Things went on so well and Belgium's newly elected executive organized the first-ever unity conference in early 2017. It brought together all stakeholders. The conference was great. Its goal was aimed to 'build a global synergy towards the restoration of the statehood of the former British Southern Cameroons.' I was very instrumental in successfully mobilizing the women and organizing and coordinating the catering services for the entire conference.

On the 22nd of September 2017, Sisiku called on all Ambazonians to come out in solidarity with the fallen heroes murdered in cold blood. Ambazonians at home and abroad took to the streets to protest. This led to the worst day of bloodshed in the revolution. There have been terrifying and horrifying moments: villages burned to the ground, hospitals destroyed, people burnt alive in their houses. The international community and media turned a blind eye to these atrocities.

On 1st October 2017, President Sisiku asked all Ambazonians, home and abroad, to come out and proclaim the restoration of their statehood. Everyone who could walk was out in the streets. But even this most special of days, our joy was snatched from us along with our compatriots murdered by soldiers of La Republique du Cameroun.

In January 2018, Sisiku Ayuk Julius Tabe, Deacon Tassang Wilfred, Pa Nfor Ngalla Nfor, Barrister Eyembe Elias, Dr. Ndeh Fidelis Che, Barrister Blaise Berinyuy, Prof Awasom, Dr. Kimeng, and Dr. Cornelius Kwanga, were abducted in Nigeria and illegally taken to French Cameroun. The international community remained silent. Despite the worldwide demonstrations and sit-in strikes by

113

Ambazonians to protest the abduction of our leaders, the international community still did nothing. The UN, Amnesty International, European Union (EU), African Union (AU), all lost their voices. At this point, the revolution seemed to lose its earlier momentum, and hope seemed to be fading fast. No one had the courage to take over and restore hope to the people.

African legend and Nobel Peace Prize winner Desmond Tutu once said:

"If you are neutral in situations of injustice, you have chosen the side of the oppressor. If an elephant has its foot on the tail of a mouse and you say that you are neutral, the mouse will not appreciate your neutrality."

Then, Dr. Sako Samuel came in. He came out more powerful than expected. He set the revolution rolling again. President Sako initiated the idea of county-by-county and LGA-by-LGA. People then became enthusiastic about the revolution, and everyone wanted to donate directly to their local government.

With the abduction of our leaders, I was voted into the Restoration Council. I accepted to serve Ambazonia even if it meant being the last man standing. For once, I could sit and listen or argue with people who have offered a lot to the Ambazonia people like Pa Augustin Ndangam. It has always been a great honor serving in that house. But let me tell you, it has never been easy because of the arguments and debates that occur in Ambazonian groups.

On 27th June 2018, I had to fly from Europe to the U.S to take part in the Ambazonia hearing at the U.S. Capitol, together with some great personalities like Pa Mola Njoh Litumbe, Mr. Elvis Kometa, Boh Herbert, Dr. Ebenezer Akwanga, and many others. It was great. I thought our case would receive the attention of the United Nations. But shockingly enough, almost one year later, no action was taken to address the nightmare unfolding in Ambazonia.

In late 2018, our abducted leaders were finally transferred from the underground jails at SED to Kondengui Central Prison in Yaoundé. There was hope for their release. But that has not become a reality.

I am ready to put in my best. I will be back to update you on the conference. But before I go, I vow to keep going in this revolution, even if I am the only one standing. I will fight until I reach Buea.

CHAPTER 15

A LETTER TO PAUL BIYA

DOROTHY MOFOR

An agreement was made before the marriage of the Southern Cameroons and French Cameroon. We got married to you, on the terms that the agreement we made was going to be fulfilled and binding. We were fine at the beginning of the agreement. We gave ourselves and our resources because we thought the relationship was amicable. We did not know that you had a different plan (to change the agreement). During Ahidjo's reign, we were treated somewhat decently for about 10 years after our wedding. When he resigned, you took over and didn't follow the marital contract. You used all of our resources; you exploited us.

We thought that you would have realized that you have been hurting us. Those resources belong to us; they were given to us by a benevolent God for us to live on. We had our bananas, and cocoa estates. We had our esteemed Ombe Technical College, rubber and oil palm plantations, tea estates in Ndu and Tole, and abundant coffee like Santa Coffee Estates. We also had viable business institutions like the Produce Marketing Boards, Cameroon Bank, and Bali and Tiko Airports.

Back then, when things were good, our children were not idle during holidays. They would go to the estates and select coffee beans. Their parents were able to sell their coffee to raise money for their education.

Every year, Mr. Paul Biya, you have made empty proclamations about changing the country and helping Anglophones. Before we joined French Cameroons, we had our own flag with our own symbol, but you ignored us. After we join you, our flag had two stars representing a husband and wife with equal powers. We believed we were a part of a federation. Alas, it was all falsehood!

Do you know that you have bitten the hand that feeds you? Since you and your people are not keeping to the terms of the agreement that was made long ago, about 60 years ago, you should leave us alone so that we can reclaim our homeland, a place which the almighty God gifted us with. You have brought war to the land of our ancestors. The God we serve will protect us.

Are you really a God-fearing man as your acolytes proclaim? Do you think that you and your soldiers are gods? Your army has killed many Southern Cameroonians. Many children: our future generations, are no more. When Southern Cameroonians speak out, they are either imprisoned or killed. What do you think you will tell God about your actions? A good President should rule his people with justice and peace."

Do you know what happened to King Nebuchadnezzar in the Bible? Do you know what happened to Pharaoh's Army? You want us to reconcile now. Are you going to bring back the souls you have exterminated? Are you going to bring back our children and our relatives! Are you going to rebuild the hospitals, the schools, and homes that you have destroyed? Can you hear the lamentations of the mothers and the groans of fathers whose children you have cut down so mercilessly?

117

I tell you, since you think you are the god of Cameroon, the Almighty God, who created the earth and its peoples, will destroy you. Your pain will be immeasurable. We will not surrender.

To the moderator of the Presbyterian Church Cameroon (PCC), the pastors, the bishops, and the cardinals of the Catholic church, the Imams: You are the shepherds. God has put in place to guide his sheep. Why can't you be brave like Prophet Elijah? The Almighty sees that His churches are empty and the congregations that used to worship Him are no more. You have scattered His sheep in all directions. The right hand of God is pointing at you!

To some of the people of the Southern Cameroons, especially those traitors who support Paul Biya because of bread crumbs; the right hand of God is pointing at you! To the commanders of Biya's army sent to kill us, the right hand of God is pointing at you! To you Mr. Biya, for the pain you have caused us, the right hand of God is pointing at you!

Yes, to all of you who have been killing us and desecrating our land. The right hand of God is pointing at you! The day of reckoning is not far away!

I must leave to go and attend to funerals. I wait!

CHAPTER 16

DIVINE REVELATION

RACHAEL ITAH-TIMA

How could it be possible that educated, knowledgeable, and talented men and women refuse to partner with those that are tirelessly, selflessly fighting and dying for an independent the Southern Cameroons? Are they blind to the reality of decades of humiliation, slavery, oppression, and assimilation of Southern Cameroonians? Blindness is not only when one is physically impaired because of the loss of sight. There is also spiritual blindness and other negative tendencies —lack of empathy, greed, and acceptance of subservience even when you matter more than the slave master.

I ask again: how can abled-bodied men and women stand by and watch, yet blatantly refuse to accept the fact that there is an on-going genocide and a scorched-earth policy being undertaken in the Southern Cameroons—our beloved Ambazonia? The day of reckoning will surely come.

Of these countless appellations—Anglo fools, Les Bamenda, Rats, Dogs, Cockroaches, L´enemies dans la Maison, Two Cubes of Sugar that refused to melt, NOSO, etc, let me ask you which of these are you familiar or can you identify with? Certainly, none, I hope.

Even as a child growing up in Yaoundé, the distinctions between Southern Cameroonians and the people of French Cameroun were

119

obvious. Every day after school we were targeted. As young as we were then, one could hear abusive comments such as "Les Anglos," "rentrez chez vous." How could we have understood that we were being referred to as strangers, in a place we considered home?

The declaration of war by Dictator Paul Biya on the people of Southern Cameroons on November 30th, 2017, was the outcome of an overdue time bomb. History never recorded a country gaining her independence with an option to, by joining an already independent nation. This was a systematically failed decolonisation endeavour. That was the case of the Southern Cameroons. A fundamental fact to be considered the major root cause of the ongoing genocide in the Southern Cameroons. The people now seek to restore their stolen independence. Their divide and rule tactics, kill some few, burn down some homes, arrest a handful and the rest will retreat to their holes, unfortunately did not work in La Republique du Cameroun´s favour this time around. The people of the Southern Cameroons are adamant. They call themselves "The never again generation."

Yes! It all continued with this generation when teachers and lawyers said enough was enough. They took to the streets in 2016 with peace messages on placards but they were abused, trampled upon, and disgraced. Students on the other hand were attacked on university campuses. They were beaten and dragged in sewage water while some were taken to unknown destinations and have not been accounted for to date. All because they demanded educational and legal reforms. Was that too much to ask for? Weh!

Today the streets of the Southern Cameroons are covered with blood. There are scenes of women digging graves and burying their dead. Others are in refugee camps in neighbouring countries, while many others are languishing in deplorable conditions in La Republic du Cameroun jails. Despite this, the people of the Southern

Cameroons have refused to give up this time. We want our country back. Trade unions started this revolution as the Consortium, a group or word Paul Biya's Cameroon had never heard of. The revolution continued with the activities of the Southern Cameroons Ambazonian Consortium United Front (SCACUF) the Governing Council and the present Interim Government. The latter has successfully put in place administrative units aimed at restoring self-governance in the Southern Cameroons as they existed before 1972. It should be noted that it was in 1972 that La Republique du Cameroun illegally annexed the Southern Cameroons.

The view that our struggle is a 'God-ordained struggle' coincides with most of my personal encounters on this journey. When each country in the diaspora with a concentration of Southern Cameroonians had to send a representative to every Department of the Interim Government, I seized the opportunity to get into the Department of Health and Social Services because I am a Social Worker with experience in conflict management and conflict resolution. After just a few days in the Department, I was assigned to support Ambazonian detainees in prisons in French Cameroun and the Southern Cameroons. On reflection, I wondered whether Almighty God was saying something to me. Coincidentally, I was the head of the prison ministry in my Local Church Community.

At a very early stage in the liberation struggle, I was confronted with the results of the brutality that our people had to put up with in French Cameroon Prisons. Their pains, from bullet wounds, broken ribs from torture, being served rotten and maggot-filled food or going for days without food, not having a comfortable space to sleep on were insufferable. In addition, complaints of 10 people packed in a 2m-by-2m room, no medical support for their injuries, and several other despicable conditions were the order of the day. Corruption amongst the detainees was equally a common problem. I had to deal with scandals of supposed prison coordinators syphoning money meant for all fellow inmates, blackmailing others and handing them over to the prison authorities, etc.

Nevertheless, I continue, documenting, raising funds to meet their needs, contacting lawyers for representation in court, contacting Partner NGOs and family members of the detainees at Kondengui Central and Principal Prisons, Douala New Bell Prison, Bamenda Central prison, Buea Central Prison Bafoussam Central Prison, Mfou Principal Prison Ntui Principal Prison, Yoko Central prison, Mbalmayo Central prison, and many other hidden detention centres. The challenge is huge dealing with more than 3000 detainees, but my resolve to accomplish this mission is immeasurable. With God's grace, I continue to stand. I, therefore, urge all Southern Cameroonians to be steadfast and focused on this challenging journey. We do not need to be preoccupied with the many conspiracy theories when so much real work needs to be done and genuine independence beckons.

Berlin! Berlin! It was recorded, in 1884, the Europeans sat in Berlin and partitioned Africa, but this time around, Ambazonians gathered in Berlin from Friday 12th-14th April 2019 for the ASSC (Ambazonia Stakeholders Strategic Conference) to seek ways forward. At a dark and confusing time when the first Interim President of Government Sisikou Julius Ayuk Tabe and his Cabinet were already under the enemy's trap in Yaoundé. Ambazonionas of all walks of life came from all over the world. I would describe this as the unforgettable gathering, as the 2nd Interim President, Dr, Samuel Ikome Sako, mustered up the courage and energy to stand up for the Ambazonian people, despite all the challenges that he confronted. It would forever be remembered that he stepped into those shoes at a very desperate time. No wonder he and his cabinet are weathering all the storms that they encountered.

The conference provided three memorable days that equipped and strengthened me to stand tall in the struggle for the long haul. My husband also attended this conference. He had so many questions on his mind about the direction, leadership, and management of our struggle. But since Berlin, he has not relented in his support for our independence struggle. Despite the resounding success of our Berlin conference, some dark clouds were evident, as some people plotted to topple the leadership of Dr Sako. It did not work. Instead, novel ideas about Ambazonia governance were developed and agreed upon for immediate implementation. For instance, the expansion and strengthening of the Restoration Council, and the emergence of the Department of Women´s Services. The Amba Peace Plan (APP), Local Government Areas and County by County structure, a bottom-up framework of governance were put in place to facilitate good practices, solid approach for accountability, local identity, and dynamic governance at the Southern Cameroons/Ambazonia´s complete restoration.

The Department of Women Services of our Interim Government was created—another indicator of how our government is responsive to the needs and representation of all Ambazonians. It is to be emphasised that the Ambazonian woman is already the most victimized and is already bearing the brunt of the war: rape, death of their husbands and children from gunshots by LRC soldiers, their homes/ villages burnt down, and many fleeing for their lives into the bushes where they resort to using moss plant as their monthly hygienic support (pads). The pregnant ones ended up giving birth to babies in the bushes without any appropriate antenatal and postnatal care. Many others are roaming the streets of neighbouring countries as refugees and others engaging in prostitution or giving birth and selling their babies just to survive.

After Sunday, April 14th, 2019, as of the Berlin Ambazonian Stakeholder's Conference, Dr. Patience Abiedu to date bares the responsibilities as first Secretary of State of Women's Services. A think tank of women was immediately set up. Groundwork for the conceptualization of projects, methods on how to handle the already deplorable situation of the Southern Cameroons Woman, gave some of us sleepless nights. I will not forget that early morning Ma Irene Ngwa, Director of Resource Mobilization in the IG with Dr. (Ma) Patience beckoned. Without any hesitation, I doubled up my role in the DWS to the existing one in HSS. These sacrifices paid off, as some months later, I was called to work closely with the secretary of state as the Chief of Staff of the Department. What can I say to all sisters tirelessly working in the background, ready to answer to every request, be it fundraising or being the voice of the voiceless Ambazonia woman? I say a big thank you to you all priceless jewels!

It´s believed that when a woman cries heaven answers quickly. The voiceless majority of the Ambazonians, especially those on Ground Zero, have been given a voice on our online Ambazonian Broadcasting Network: "the ABC: Amba TV—The Horizon "The Voice of the Ambazonian Woman on ABC TV" was developed as a vehicle to bring hope to situations of hopelessness. The sun appearing above the horizon is symbolic of a positive outlook for our liberation struggle. The voice of the Ambazonia Woman is regularly aired on ABC Amba TV on Fridays @ 6 pm Amba time. As the first host of the program, I coordinate discussions and debates on aspects of our liberation struggle. I am grateful for this invaluable and everlasting experience and the opportunity to serve my country. The best moments are when people, especially in Ground Zero share their worries, concerns, and suggestions via WhatsApp calls during the program. I have enjoyed the good company and insights of all the women and departmental panellist. I thank you all for the patriotic support.

Desperate moments call for desperate actions. The Ambazonian Woman is born with a generous heart. The desire to put smiles on the faces of our fallen hero widows, resulted into the realization of the Southern Cameroons Widows Empowerment Program (SCWEP). This sustainable humanitarian program assists women, especially widows. This initiative seeks to empower these women to rejuvenate their lives. The token material support provided through this initiative is nothing compared to the women's losses. But we have taken the first baby steps. We plan to do better things for our Heroes' Widows. We know and accept that they are our eternal responsibility. Therefore, we will always come knocking at the doors of sympathizers, for support and kindness.

Good and sustained collaboration can take us closer to our goal. Thanks to the women in the Ambazonian Coalition Team who have a defined goal—to facilitate mediation. Partnering with the ACT and the Department of Women Services of the Interim Government led to the creation of the Women for Permanent Peace and Justice group/platform. This led to the first-ever women's conference with the gracious and high-profile participation of women freedom fighters with experience of struggle for self-determination. That was a great event. It was motivational and an eye-opener for determined Ambazonian women. Congratulations to Ma E. Osong, Ma P. Abiedu Ma B. Teboh, and many of us. Through this, the need for capacity and civil society building to enhance the role of women in the Ambazonia Liberation has become more urgent and significant.

Could I have stayed this long in the Liberation Struggle recalling every challenge along this journey? Glory be to God Almighty who showed up that night in March 2018 after soaking myself in my own tears seeking for and demanding what would become of the Southern Cameroons? Alas! just like in Prophet Ezekiel´s visions, the heavens opened. With two windows one scary face shouting and spitting out fire on Ambazonians, at a point, people started giving up. And behold, the Divine revelation was made known to me. The second window was opened with a flying Ambazonian flag accompanied with golden rays and a voice assuring us that the road maybe rough and dreary, but He will sound the trumpets of victory in His own Time… Praise the Lord.

Whether the enemy likes it or not the Southern Cameroons shall be free.

CHAPTER 17

AMBAZONIA – THIS IS MY STORY

EMMA ENDELEY

Aunty, I never knew you were such a politician, getting into Cameroon's politics,". my nephew said. I kept looking at him as he said, "They created the problem by making us join LRC. Let them solve the problem." My jaw dropped on this quiet Sunday in 2018, as we were having a family dinner to celebrate our multiple birthdays that fell in January and February. This was the first time my jaw dropped in shock and amazement. It will come to drop many more times in the coming years. I might need a wheelbarrow to pick up and load all the dropped jaws.

Before 2018, I had never heard of the marching by lawyers, teachers, and the population with leaves and branches which indicated the protest was peaceful. I remember it was my cousin, who is a lawyer, that informed me about the lawyers strike in 2017. I was visiting Cameroon at the time and did not realize anything was going on. I was just happy to spend some time with him during my visit.

As I continued to follow what was happening in the Southern Cameroons, I could not believe my eyes and ears. I began to learn the history of my people which I had not been taught in school in Cameroon. I went to primary school in the 1960s. All I remember of Cameroon's history as a pre-teen was hearing my father talk of the maquisards[4] and terrorists. Someone was killing the Bamilekes, cutting their heads and lining the heads along the highway. This was déjà vu… Fast forward to 2018! Kill Amba boys and label them terrorists. Kill unarmed men, boys, old men, women, and children and label them terrorists! Even as a child, I knew a paralyzing fear had gripped the English-speaking population around Kumba, Tombel area. A lot of the villagers had run to Buea, Muyuka, Tiko, Victoria, and Kumba to escape the violence. As time went on, my jaw dropped a few times as I started dotting the i's and crossing the t's of what was unfolding in the country.

I could now answer my nephew's questions and suggestions to me about the struggle. I answered the first question. I said, "Son, this is not politics. The government of LRC has declared war on my people and continues to kill my people on the scale of genocide and ethnic cleansing. The word AMBA was a label they gave to those they killed or threw in jail. I told my nephew this is not politics; this is life and death. I asked him to follow the struggle on the internet and to read what is going on. Of course, there was a gag on the media as LRC tried to cover up the atrocities they were committing. They blocked internet access, they collected people's phones at random to see what they were reading or watching. They hoped to cover their tracks of the genocide they were committing. The population was so paralyzed with fear that they could not report the disappearances of their family members. Some were in jail, torture chambers or mass graves which we are yet to find and to account for all the missing persons," I said. I told my nephew, "No, I am not playing politics. I am watching my people facing life and death, targeted killings, illegal

---

[4] Marquisards: Cameroonian armed forces notoriously known for brutalizing and killing members of the Bamilike ethnic group of the West Region of La Republique du Cameroon between the 1950s and 1960s.

and forced imprisonments, killing in detention centers and torture chambers."

I could not handle it. To keep my sanity, I could only do what I could as the spirit led me. I have met a few close relatives who tell me they do not want to get involved in politics and I should respect their political affiliations. I wondered what political affiliations those are. Is killing your brother, neighbor, father, uncle, grandma, politics? Is that the case according to the ruling party CPDM with its almost ninety-year-old president, who has been in power for forty years and still counting? A president who declared war on his unarmed population! No, that is not politics and no justification for killing a people who just asked that their statehood be restored, because they were tired of being marginalized in their own land. Is that a reason to kill them? Of course, the real agenda of LRC has since unfolded as the war has taken a more gruesome and sinister course.

The second question or suggestion is that it is their war for selling us out to the French instead of joining Nigeria as Dr. E. M. L. Endeley had suggested. There comes a time in this life when the circumstances of the present have to force you to look beyond the past to be able to handle the present. It is not amid gunshots, burning our villages, raping our young girls and women, killing our sons, ages 12 to 40, that we will stand paralyzed on the spot saying it was Foncha's fault. The enemy is killing Foncha's relatives and kinsmen. The enemy is killing Endeley's kinsmen as well. This is definitely not the time to figure out who betrayed whom and why. We need to unite against our common enemy French Cameroun. At this time, however, the enemy is trying to hold on to its divide and rule *modus operandum*, one of its sinister plans to keep the territory in perpetual bondage.

Growing up as a child, and well into my teens, I knew that my father, a postmaster, worked in all the regions of the Southern Cameroons—from the rolling hills and grasslands of Nkambe, Bamenda, and Wum, to the forest and brown hills of Meme, the seaside towns of Tiko, Victoria, and Buea at the foot of the majestic Mount Fako, he was the postmaster. He opened all the post offices and postal departments in all of the Southern Cameroons. When LRC took over all our institutions, my father was sent to Yaoundé to set up the Postal Directorate. They could not understand his work ethic. He was amazed at their few working hours, as many of them did not return to work after their lunch of bagette, miondo, bobolo, wine, and taking a siesta. One thing that stood out was, instead of assimilating the 9 to 5 work ethic, many were determined to promote their laid-back lifestyle with corruption galore.

I always quote the handling of life after work which perpetrates the corrupt system of "chop broke pot[5]." There was no pension or social security system set up to take care of you after you retire. That was why the government officials never want to retire, including the president, Paul Biya. They work until they die in office at age ninety or more. Hence the systematic riddance of the young people who might take over their jobs someday! Young people are therefore left jobless. This began the great exodus of Cameroon's youth. Many of them end up in the cold dark waters of the Red Sea. Others ending in the damp, wet forests of South America amidst snakes, crocodiles, and other wild animals! The old Beti, Bulu, Ewondo, Sawa, and CPDM groups in all the regions of the country continue to cling to power, reducing their legal ages when necessary.

Going back to my comparison of the two systems of work

---

[5] Chop broke pot: A Cameroonian Pidgin phrase which means to act recklessly, without thinking of the future. Literally translates as "to eat and break the pot".

ethics—I worked in Cameroon, and I worked in Nigeria which also has the British work ethic. My father died in 1975 after he retired as a postal director. His pension or benefits were never paid. I worked in Cameroon. I was actually the first television trained journalist from 1977 to 1978 when I returned with a master's degree in radio-television production. I worked in radio Buea station for three years and had to leave for health reasons. I got hired next door in Nigerian Television Authority. When I left Cameroon after working for three years, I was still on a temporary salary known in French as 'avance de solde.' That system only exists in the French colonies. When I moved over to Nigeria, I got my full salary every month from day one. When I left and went on voluntary retirement at age 42, (you could go on voluntary retirement after working for ten years) your pension kicks in when you turn 45. On my 45th birthday, my pension was in my account, and it has never stopped. That is what I call a system that works. For years, I kept going to Yaoundé to get my father's pension for his widow and young children. It never came.

So, I tell my nephews, my taking part in this struggle goes beyond me. It is for your children and my grandchildren. It is leaving the darkness and moving into the light. The French or francophone system is the embodiment of darkness, corruption, inefficiency, and greed. We need to go back to the light—the British efficient system which holds everyone accountable, rewards hard work, and condemns corruption and bribery. In the French system, you must bribe your way from desk to desk to get one document signed. If you do not pay a bribe, you don't get the service you desire. To uproot this system, we need a restoration of our independence, nothing more nothing less. The French system in LRC can never change. They can wallow in their inefficiency and corruption. The Southern Cameroons will return to its past glory. France benefits from the corrupt leaders who give them free license to rape and plunder her colonies.

That is why we are determined to fight until the last man standing. The alternative is decadence, corruption, continuous brain-drain with our youths dying en route to a greener pasture. The Southern Cameroons, Ambazonia is the only green pasture we need. We have the manpower and the savvy to build our nation and no one should compare us to Southern Sudan. We learn from the mistakes of others. Compare us to Rwanda, we will accept that. Ambazonia rise, rise to fall no more! Long live the Federal Republic of Ambazonia, short live the struggle. I am Fako, I am Southern Cameroon, I am Ambazonia.

I cannot end this chapter without writing an open letter to Paul Biya and copy Chantal Biya and Emmanuel Macron:

Dear Mr. Paul Biya,

Please give a copy of this letter to your wife Chantal and one to Mr. Emmanuel Macron of France, who provides you with the funds to kill Southern Cameroonians and encourages you to scorch the earth of Southern Cameroons like they did in Haiti, burning everything in their path.

This is not the first time you and your predecessor Ahmadou Ahidjo have launched genocide against your citizens. You killed the Bamilekes and the Bassas, who were the opposition party. That was the first genocide in Cameroon. Now you are killing and launching genocide on the peace-loving people of the Southern Cameroons Ambazonia. Have you not spilled enough blood? Even giant bloodsuckers get full. Is the oil that flows under Ambazonia soil worth killing all of us for? Are the mineral deposits, our rich timber-filled forests a reason to wipe us out? You, your son, and your cronies have been collecting free-of-charge our timber, our crude oil, our fruits, our

132

fish, everything given by God to the people of Ambazonia. You left the territory ten times worse than you found it in 1961. When is enough, enough for you? You have sons and at least one daughter that we know. She and her brothers are born to parents—you and Chantal. You have ordered the killing of over 10,000 young people. Your unprofessional soldiers have killed babies, suckling babies, old women, children sleeping; they have burnt villages, over 300 of them. I ask you again Mr. Paul Biya, when is enough, enough?

You can stop this war by calling off your dogs that thoughtlessly kill innocent civilians by taking part in the Swiss talks. Hello! That single act will save your people and La Republique du Cameroun— your country from total collapse. Mr. Macron, in the name of your stepchildren, stop giving Paul Biya the money and tools to kill my people! France has collected our oil at ridiculously low prices and our cocoa to make your beautiful chocolate treats. Must you wipe us out of this world so that the French can maintain their lifestyles? Emmanuel Macron, the color of the blood of our children is the same as your children and Biya's children. Chantal, you and the first lady of France carried your babies for nine months just like the mothers of the children massacred in their sleep in Ngarbuh. Biya and Macron, the greatest cowards in the world are afraid to sit down at the table in Switzerland to negotiate a just peace and separation. Be a man, Paul Biya, for once in your wretched life, and call off this war so that we can go our separate ways. Stop the carnage, stop the genocide. Mr. Macron, be a man and make your puppet do the right thing. The blood of all those killed, maimed, and rotting in jail are on your heads Mr. and Mrs. Biya and Mr. and Mrs. Emmanuel Macron. Do the right thing.

Sincerely,

An Ambazonian Mother

CHAPTER 18

CONCEALING THE GENOCIDE

RACHAEL ITAH-TIMA

Mamma (not her name) 29, is in prison. Until 2 years ago, Mamma had her hairdressing business, which supported her daughter, 3 siblings, and her ailing mother. The day came when she had to go into hiding because a soldier had been killed in self-defence (by restoration fighters), and she was suspected of having provided cover for the attack.

Their home was raided in the early hours of dawn. Assumed to be her, bullets rained on her elder sister and one of her brothers. They both died. Her mother was so severely beaten that when she recovered, she was crippled and mentally deranged and now no one knows of her whereabouts. Mamma's orphaned niece, although only in her pubescence, cares for the daughter, 4, while she and the other surviving brother were lucky to have been spared execution when the soldiers caught up with them.

A people previously with self-rule have progressively been reduced to being spoken to in a foreign language in their hospitals, courts, public services, and at innumerable roadblocks throughout their territory. They have been tormented by soldiers at checkpoints, who after bribery and harassment, suddenly allow them to continue on their journeys. Nelson Mandela once said, "To deny people their Human Rights is to challenge their very humanity." Since the fall of

2016, the human rights situation in the Southern Cameroons has drastically worsened. Lawyers had requested that government rescind its policy of assimilation in the courts, wherein French-speaking magistrates would preside over courts in the English-speaking regions—thereby imposing the French language on the proceedings and court participants (who were already used to the ways of British colonialists). To their dismay, lawyers were publicly humiliated and brutalized. Their pleas for certain laws to be translated into English had been ignored for decades despite incessant reminders, depicting an attitude of disregard, and forced assimilation. When students rose to protest the corrupt practices at the university where authorities had been illegally imposing and were collecting fees, the military was called in order to disperse them, causing fear of terror in the process.

Teachers did not sit on the sidelines. They too had their own grievances. The assimilation process by the government had meant that just like in the law courts, Francophone teachers who could not speak standard English were being sent to teach in Anglophone primary and secondary schools. The school curricula no longer reflected the specificity of the English-speaking region, though our people had been assured that our education would not be tempered with. The English language, although an official language in Cameroon, was being treated like a mere formality. So, just as their colleagues of the other professions had done, the teachers too joined the demonstrations. The Anglophone population gave its approval and supported all the segments to come together in a Consortium to negotiate with the government.

In a country with a poor human rights index, stemming from its colonial past, the government's response to the protests fit the well-known pattern of resolving political issues using force. This terror-based governance reached a new low when the fabric of the country's colonial past was put into question and by extension, so was the legitimacy of the government.

A consensus could not be reached, and the government was offered the possibility of allowing the Southern Cameroonian region to revert to managing its affairs as it had done independence from 1961 up until the unification in 1972. However, in January 2017, the Cameroonian government concluded that there was no point offering carrots anymore and resorted to the stick. Supposed and suspected leaders were arrested. Protests erupted and the armed forces expanded the use of lethal force. Those who were arrested are currently being tortured and detained under very inhumane conditions, living in dungeons-like interments. Along with protracted incommunicado, many detainees have also been tortured to death.

Unfortunately, it has become a continuous practice for BIR soldiers to chase and kill suspected restoration activists all over the country, which is how the refugee and an internally displacement crisis has precipitated. Still, the government would not back down. So too did the activists in detention, in exile, and on the run; they still held on to their demands for restoration of statehood—which put their lives in danger. Soon, everyone in the English-speaking region became a suspect for anything deemed not palatable to the government and the broad sweeping anti-terrorism law of 2014 was invoked. All those arrested were suddenly terrorists and liable to the death penalty. Tired of being chased around, arrested, brutalized, raped, and released from police custody only after the payment of exorbitant bribes, some youth took up self-defense. After all, Hon. Joseph Wirba had reminded everyone in his 2016 speech at the National Assembly that "When injustice becomes law, resistance becomes a duty."

The media's hateful language against supposed Anglophone "terrorists" amplified and gave President Biya a pretext to declare war—which he did on November 30, 2017. The jails were already filled. Biya's soldiers would surround villages, pillage them, and burn them to the ground, which included the humble habitations of subsistence farmers. While Biya's army generals claim on record that the army only incinerates houses they suspect to have weapons in them, there are countless videos and photos to disprove such statements. Also, on countless occasions, unsuspecting young males would be executed on the streets in broad daylight, for apparently no other reason than to shock and terrorize Anglophone communities. On other occasions, there have been cases of targeted extrajudicial killings that even the USA Ambassador to Cameroon has decried.

With a military that has gone on the rampage, criminals saw their field day too to participate in the spoils.

Since the declaration of war, the region of the former British Southern Cameroons has become a lawless enclave where soldiers, restoration of independence forces, rogues, and those whose identities mutate amongst these groups, fight to gain control, often at the detriment of an innocent and unarmed population. A key example of this would be the Ngarbuh Massacre. At 5 am on February 14th, 2020, BIR soldiers aided by government militia, descended on the small village of Ngarbuh, in Donga Mantung County, after they were suspected of harbouring restorationist fighters. Paul Biya's soldiers killed people, 14 of them children and one pregnant woman! Thus, the woman and children bear the brunt of this genocidal war, according to the UN Human Rights watch.

When brutal fighting displaces hundreds of thousands of

civilians, it usually sets international alarm bells ringing. But this does not seem to apply to Cameroon. There is no mediation, no large relief programme, no media interest, and little pressure applied on the parties to stop attacking civilians. The explanation for this most likely lies in the unbalanced alliance between corrupt governments in poor countries rich in natural resources and multinational companies from technologically advanced rich countries.

Whatever the reasons for concealing or neglecting this genocide, Southern Cameroonians will continue to proclaim: "injustice anywhere is injustice everywhere" until truth and justice prevail and are revealed!

CHAPTER 19

BYE BYE, DICTATOR BIYA

MARY MUMA

You had been an unwelcome guest in our land

We tolerated your temper, your tantrums, and your trickery

You foolishly misunderstood us for underlings

You stuffed yourself with our food, our wine, our honey,

and made yourself the landlord of our God-given land

One day you ran amok and killed your host's sons

Because they dared to dismiss you from their home

You violated his daughters and his wife

You even invited other strangers to come and have a go

Your host dared not open his mouth

He begged you to leave; you had had your fill, or had you?

His neighbour's family are no more

He begs you to let him go bury the dead

You refuse; he's your prisoner, your host.

But the Townspeople had not seen your host for a long time

They rallied to his front door.

You barred the entrance.

They sent volleys through the window

The cannon popped, shattering the door

You escape through the backdoor, wounded

If the bullet wounds do not kill you,

Your natural infirmity will;

The choice is not yours to make.

Your end is nigh.

Reason—You have done the unthinkable

You have traded good with evil

You cannot escape God's wrath.

Pride, arrogance, bribery, debauchery will not save you

You live on a ventilator of borrowed time

Got away with borrowed trillions from

'Chinada' and 'Franceland.'

As your sun sets, Ambazonia's is rising,

scattering the rays of freedom

to bring back the lushness of the vegetation

which carpets our homeland.

Your fate is that of dictators of not-too-distant memory

They too went under.

Nothing could save them when the bell tolled;

Not even the menacing guards

 and the praise-singing sycophants

– Anglophone and Francophone,

the maggots who leak your smelly wounds

to remain mindless errand boys.

So, bye bye on your homeward journey to meet your maker

So, Bye Bye, from Ambazonia. We part ways.

We reclaim our homes, our land, our royalty, and our laughter.

You will crave precious drops of the clear water from the fountains of Mount Fako and the glorious milk from our cows at Tadu as you flounder in the eternal furnace of Hell.

BYE BYE to Etoudi

Definitions and Key Terms

AIP – Acting Interim President of Southern Cameroons

APLM- African People's Liberation Movement

APPG- All-Party Parliamentary Groups

ASSC – Ambazonia Stakeholders Strategic Conference

BIR – Rapid Intervention Battalion Brigade

CCAST Bambili – Cameroon College of Arts Science and Technology

COS – Chief of Staff

CPDM – Cameroon People's Democratic Movement

ENAM – Ecole Nationale D'Administration Et De Magistrature

FRA – Federal Republic of Ambazonia

GTC Ombe – Government Technical College

HSS – Health and Social Services

LRC- La Republique du Cameroun

"Les Anglos" – (in French) a shortened version "le anglophones" or "the anglophones" referring to the English-Speaking population of Cameroon.

LGA – Local Government Area

MIDENO- North-West Development Authority

MoRISC – Movement for the Restoration of the Independence of Southern Cameroons

MP – Member of Parliament

NERA-10 – The 10 Ambazonians abducted from the Nera Hotel in Nigeria

NOSO – An abbreviation for "North-West" & "South-West ", which are the two regions that make up the Southern Cameroons.

PCC – Presbyterian Church Cameroon

PWD – Public Works Department

"Rentrez chez vous"- return to your home

SCACUF -Southern Cameroons Ambazonia Consortium United Front

SCNC Southern Cameroons National Council

SCWEP- Southern Cameroons Widow's Empowerment Program

SED State Defense Secretariat

SOCADEF – Southern Cameroons Defense Forces

SOS –Secretary of State

Takembeng – A female social movement from the North-West region of the Southern Cameroons.

UNGA – United Nations General Assembly

WADA-Water and Development Alliance

Historical of Timeline of the Southern Cameroons

1884: The Berlin Conference is overseen by Otto Von Bismarck. Africa is partitioned and Cameroon becomes a German Colony.

1911 to 1916: Germany loses the first war, resulting in the loss of its African colonies, including Kamerun—which made up of present-day Cameroon, parts of Eastern Nigeria, parts of Northern

1916: Following the end of German rule, the colony is divided into two new colonies: the British Cameroons and French Cameroon,

1946 to 1953: The Southern Cameroons (a UN class B Trust Territory) is governed by the British High Commission in Nigeria, with representatives in the Nigerian Eastern House of Assembly.

1953: The Southern Cameroons Representatives walked out en-masse in protest from the Eastern House of Assembly in Enugu.

1953 to 1961: The Southern Cameroons is a self-governing territory, with a Prime Minister, Cabinet, and Capital seated in Buea. (Dr. Emmanuel Endeley as first Premier)

1955: The KNDP (Kamerun National Democratic Party) is formed, inspired by re-unification sympathizers. John Ngu Foncha is made leader of the party.

1957: London Constitutional Conference increased the number of elected members of the House from 13 to 26 and created a house of Chiefs for prominent traditional rulers.

1959: The Southern Cameroons organized democratic elections for a third time and effected the first peaceful and democratic transfer of power in sub-Saharan Africa.

1960: The United Nations impose the Two Alternatives on The Southern Cameroons: "independence by joining" either La Republique du Cameroun or the Federal Republic of Nigeria

January 1, 1960: La Republique du Cameroon gains its independence from France.

February 11, 1961: The Southern Cameroons voted in an UN-organized plebiscite to have its independence from Britain in a defined union with LRC.

October 1, 1961, Britain ceased to be the Colonial Master of the Southern Cameroons. J.O. Field was the "Handing Over" officer. Southern Cameroons was to be officially declared an independent state, to assert its future. At Bongo Square in Buea, the Union Jack was lowered, instead of French East Cameroon and the Southern Cameroons sitting down to work out a treaty of Union, Ahidjo's sent in the Gendarmes, raising the "Green, Red and Yellow" flag and Foncha was helpless. The Southern Cameroons is federated with la Republique du Cameroun as an autonomous state of West Cameroon.

September 1966: Dissolution of all political parties by President Ahmadou Ahidjo and creation of one party, the Cameroon National Union (CNU)

May 20, 1972: Federal Republic of Cameroon becomes United Republic of Cameroon orchestrated by Ahidjo

End of federation unconstitutionally with West Cameroon split into

North West and South West - the 9th and 10th Provinces of La Republique du Cameroun (beginning of annexation of the Former British Southern Camerouns)

February 1984: Country's name changes from the United Republic of Cameroon

to the Republic of Cameroon (La Republique du Cameroun) under President Paul Biya (completion of annexation)

1993: Emergence of the Southern Cameroons Liberation Movements, and the arrest and detention of Fon Gorgi Dinka

April-May 1993: The first All Anglophone Conference (AAC 1) takes place in Buea, Cameroon

The Buea Declaration issued calling for constitutional amendments to restore the 1961 federation

April-May 1994: The second All Anglophone Conference 11

(AAC II) takes place in Bamenda, Cameroon

The Bamenda Proclamation issued, demanding the declaration of independence if federation is not restored within a reasonable time

May 20, 2010: UN representative, Ali Triki, who is the President of the 64th General Assembly of the UN, hand's over to Paul Biya, Cameroun's Head of State, two maps during the celebration of Cameroon's 50th Anniversary. Ali Triki declared "*Voici les cartes de Cameroon Britannique. Referring to the map of the Southern Cameroons.*

October 2016: Lawyers and Teachers protest over government use French civil law over common law and French teachers in English schools

September 22, 2017: peaceful protests all over the Southern Cameroons (Ambazonia) denouncing the continued colonization and illegal occupation of their land

October 1st, 2017: Restoration of the Independence of the Southern Cameroons

November 30, 2017: President Paul Biya of la Republic du Cameroun waged war on the Southern Cameroons

Reference

www.ambazoniagenocidelibrary.com

Your Thoughts

_____

_____

_____

_____

_____

_____

_____

_____

_____

_____

_____

_____

_____

_____

_____

_____

Your Thoughts

_____

_____

_____

_____

_____

_____

_____

_____

_____

_____

_____

_____

_____

_____

Made in the USA
Columbia, SC
10 November 2021

48599965R00088